YC
Kεr
TO
HAPPINESS

Harold Sherman

Square Circles Publishing

YOUR KEY TO HAPPINESS
by Harold Sherman

SQUARE CIRCLES PUBLISHING
P. O. Box 9682, Pahrump, NV 89060
www.SquareCircles.com

ISBN: 978-0-9893962-5-7
eISBN: 978-0-9856176-5-3

When my father wrote *Your Key to Happiness* in 1935, I was a happy little six-year-old, with a life-time of new experiences stretching out before me.

Now, I am approaching the twilight years of that lifetime and fully realize the power that we each have within us to control our lives in a positive way.

My Dad was a man "ahead of his time" in so many areas. However, the principles he incorporated in this book, many years ago, can be used just as effectively in today's world.

MARCIA SHERMAN LYNCH
March 2012

may your lives
be filled with increasing
happiness through the
years! Best wishes!
Sincerely

Contents

To You—
Who Are About to
Read This Book

*T*here is much very much, I would like to say to you, could I meet and talk personally with you, who are about to read this book. But perhaps, if you will let yourself feel that I am talking to you now, alone, we can have a good visit together.

I have been asked by so many thousands of men and women, as the result of my radio talks on personal philosophy, how I came to believe, as I do, in the power of right thinking and the unquestioned existence of a personal God, that I feel this will be one of your first questions, too.

You have a right to ask me this question for you are a searcher after truth, as am I, and you have sought the answer to these age-old and perplexing problems in your life. Each seeker brings to the quest his own degree of belief or skepticism, based upon the nature of his past experience. While we of today have been told that "faith is the substance of things unseen," few of us are willing to accept the evidence of faith unless we can see its works. Whatever your belief, or lack of belief, either in higher powers within yourself, or in a direct personal relation to God, you do not want to be deluded.

This was my own attitude, years ago. Certain unusual mental experiences had come to me which I could not explain in accordance with my youthful concept of this material world. It seemed fantastic and impossible, for instance, though radio was then being talked about, that human thought could ever be transmitted from one mind to another. And yet, there had been forced upon me several startling and undeniable evidences that my mind had received such thoughts. I was greatly disturbed by these happenings and found that I could confide them to few people for fear of being considered on the fringe of lunacy or placed in the category of an "abnormal child" who was subject to hallucinations.

The experiences impressed me so deeply, however, that I resolved to spend my life, devoting all the time I could possibly afford, in a study of these strange and little-understood faculties of mind, with the hope that I might, at least, clarify for myself what these mental processes were which sometimes operated beyond the so-called normal. I thought the answer might be found in the religions and philosophies of the world, and so I began a study of them. I found much of inspiration but little of illumination. I became more and more certain that the spiritual principles uniformly extolled in these various beliefs and philosophic concepts concealed great demonstrable truths.

But how could I ever get at them and reduce them to such a simple and workable formula that I could prove these principles in my everyday life? When I sought the answer in the psychic field, I found myself venturing upon ground that scientists either feared or disdained to tread. It is only in recent years that the study of what is now called "extrasensory perception" has been taken up by such eminent investigators as Dr. J. B. Rhine, of Duke University, and Dr. Gardner Murphy, formerly head of the Parapsychology Department of Columbia University. These men, modern pioneers in the field of research, are still facing the ridicule of many fellow scientists but their contributions to the definitely growing knowledge of the higher faculties of mind already loom large. They are being joined by increasing numbers of scientists, research workers, electrical engineers, astronomers, and distinguished men and women in all walks of life who are giving testimony to the existence of these powers which I sensed as a boy.

You have felt flashes of these same higher forces within you, from time to time. We all have. But we have set them down to "coincidence" or a "hunch" or the work of intuition. Fortunately, for all ordinary intents and purposes, we are insulated from the automatic operation of these higher powers of mind. Our conscious mind, which deals strictly with our five physical senses, sees to that. We have trained our conscious mind to believe that these higher powers do not exist and that we cannot come by any knowledge unless it is brought to us through one or more of these senses—sight, hearing, taste, touch and smell.

It is usually only when something of serious emotional moment happens to a close friend or loved one that sufficient intensity of thought energy is created to transmit a message to our minds against the resistance of this conscious mind. This accounts for many men and women declaring that they knew when some dear one was taken suddenly ill or met with an accident or died. They still, perhaps, did not believe in telepathy or any kind of a "psychic manifestation" and offered an apology when telling of the incident, but could give no explanation.

These were the kind of happenings, among others, for which I had to determine the answer in order to gain peace of mind. *If telepathy* and these other uncharted powers of mind were really a fact, then it would indicate that man, himself, was more than a physical being; that perhaps the great religions and philosophies of the world spoke the truth when they declared that man was also spirit.

This is not the time or place for me to take you with me on the long and soul-trying years of investigation and research and personal experimentation I gladly entered upon in the belief that, if these powers did actually exist, any persevering human should be able to prove them in his own life and with his own mind.

This book, which you now hold in your hands, was written by me at the conclusion of my search, after I had become convinced that I stood upon a firm foundation and that, insofar as I had been able to go, I knew the way and could trace and retrace my steps. I wrote this book first as a means of crystallizing for myself the knowledge which had come to me through tested life experience. The information herein contained has nothing to do with telepathy. It deals strictly with another phase of these higher faculties of mind—a great, God-given, creative power which exists within your subconscious mind and which you can learn to draw upon to bring you the things in life you most desire.

Two years after this volume was first published, I entered into a five months' series of experiments in long-distance telepathy with the Arctic explorer, Sir Hubert Wilkins. It was the first time I had attempted such work under scientific observation and, of course, I could not guarantee what results might be obtained. Wilkins was three thousand miles away in the Far North, searching for the lost Russian fliers, and I was then in my apartment in New York City.

Three nights a week, at the prearranged time of 11:30 to 12 midnight, I made my mind receptive, by a method I had developed through years of private experimenting, and attempted to receive impressions from the mind of Wilkins as to what had happened to him that day, or was happening to him, at that very moment. When each night's session was over, I typed copies of what had seemed to "come through" and mailed them to different, interested, scientific witnesses, one of whom was Dr. Gardner Murphy. Wilkins kept a diary and log and when the hundreds of impressions, recorded by me, were ultimately checked, an astonishing number of them was found to be highly accurate. The complete story of these experiments is now a part of another book, Thoughts Through Space, written with Sir Hubert Wilkins.

These experiments revealed to me much additional unexpected knowledge concerning the nature and operation of higher consciousness in man. What I was able to accomplish, I firmly believe that you or any other person of good mind, who is willing to put forth the same effort, could reasonably duplicate. My interest in telepathy and this type of mental phenomena is strictly scientific. I see no purpose being served through those who make a parlor game of it. We still do not know enough about these particular faculties of mind to take them so lightly or to experiment indiscriminately. I mention this work, simply to indicate to you the enormous possibilities ahead of evolving man.

Because you are living essentially in this physical world, you are naturally interested in learning all you can about yourself which has practical, everyday value. A most pressing question you want answered is whether or not you do possess a power within yourself capable of solving all life's problems and whether or not this power is really a part of the greatest power that ever is or ever can be—the power of God.

These questions I can answer for you because I have traveled the road of investigation you too might have wished to travel could life have afforded you that opportunity. What I say to you in every sentence in this book, I say with all the conviction of my being, and with the desire to pass on to you whatever truth I have gained and been able to prove.

So, now that we have become acquainted, let us explore ourselves together.

We are all a part of this great, wonderful, universal scheme of things. Your birth, your being here on earth, wasn't an accident however accidental it may have seemed. Remember this: You are something—and something cannot come from nothing. You must have existed in some form before you were born or you couldn't be here today. And you did exist although you are not conscious of this fact; but you existed in the Mind of the great Infinite Intelligence—God, your Father.

Don't try to understand God. We haven't any words in any language that can possibly describe to our limited intelligence what God really is. This is not the way to try to get an idea of God. But you can be sure that this vast Intelligence we call God is a Personal Being. And how can you be sure of all this? Because everything in the universe—everything on earth—has personality, identity, individuality. There is not a leaf on any tree which is exactly similar to any other leaf on any other tree of the countless trees in all the forests. Each leaf has some slight little difference which distinguishes it from all others. The same is true of the trillions upon trillions of snowflakes which blanket so much of the earth in our winter seasons. You've seen the photographed and beautifully magnified designs of these individual snowflakes. Haven't you marveled at the forces of nature which could have created these amazingly intricate designs, seemingly on the spur of the moment, when cold currents of air, rushing together in the heavens, caused moisture to freeze and take on these white flaky forms!

Examine everything about you. You will find no exact similarity anywhere. What does this prove? It proves that this is not a carbon-copy universe. No duplicates are being created. Everything, no matter how seemingly trivial or insignificant to us, is an original—it has never existed before in just exactly this form and design and appearance. It will never exist again in just this way. Do you begin to see what I mean when I say that you are just as important to this great scheme of things as any other human on earth?

You were created for a definite purpose. It was intended that you were to have a definite place to fill in life. It is up to you to find that place. You have been created a creature of free will. This God-power within you is not going to compel you to do what you came into this world with the opportunity of doing. You must discover what this is and decide to put forth the effort to do it yourself.

The reason the world is in its present state of threatened chaos is because so many humans have failed to find their destined purpose in life. If you're unhappy, if you feel you've been making no progress, if you look upon your life as a failure, if you can see little hope for the future, then you haven't yet found your individual pattern in God's great plan. I tell you positively that your pattern is there and that your inner self contains the knowledge of this pattern and will reveal it to you once you look within yourself for the right answer

Up to now you may not have realized that there was, and is, a Higher Intelligence within your own mind which can guide you. You've looked everywhere else for the answer to your problems in life but within yourself. I told you a moment ago that you can never describe God, the Great Intelligence, in words, but I say to you now, you can feel His Presence in your own mind and heart and once you sense the Presence it will be an undeniable, unmistakable experience and you will then know, beyond any shadow of a doubt, that you are never alone and that you have with you, at all times, all the power and wisdom you need to carry you happily and successfully along life's rough road.

No one exactly resembling you in physical body or personality has ever existed before in all the countless ages of the past with all the trillions of human creatures who have lived. And no one ever again, in all the countless ages to come, and with all the trillions upon trillions of humans yet to be born, will ever exactly resemble you in physical appearance or personality. I want you to think of this great fact for a moment.

All of the unhappy experiences you have had up to this present instant have been brought about because you have either not been calling upon this power within or you have been misusing it. It's through this life experience that you've been supposed to be awakened to the great possibilities within you. If you've reacted wrongly to what has happened to you—

if you've blamed these things upon others or circumstances seemingly beyond your control—then you've not yet learned that there is a higher, finer way of doing things. Until you do learn, you are going to attract, through your own wrong thinking, many more wrong, unhappy happenings.

So, get busy on yourself. You are the one person for whom you are entirely responsible. Your world, your life can be better only if you make it so. As you improve yourself, you influence all others around you. Keep in mind that you came into this life with a purpose to perform. You can't find that true purpose until you put aside your hates and bitter feelings.

There is going to come a time, within the next few years, when for you to persist in hating your fellow man, will be to put you out of step with all progress and with the laws of God as they were intended to operate on this earth. The happy, successful men and women in that day will be those who have learned to harness the God-power within them, to unite this Power, harmoniously, one with the other, to the end that the good of all may be served. This day is not so far distant as it may seem.

It makes no difference what age you are—you're going to have an individual part in this new world if you waken to the spirit of God within you and let this spirit express through you. When this happens, you'll not only get along with others, but you'll have the understanding to get along with yourself.

These thoughts may seem new to you but what I am saying is what ministers and educators and scientists are saying to you in a different way. At last, we humans are to know the real truth about ourselves and this truth is going to make us free, eventually, in body and in spirit. I urge you to accept what I have said on faith until you can prove the truth of it in your own life through the experiences I know you can attract by right thinking.

Remember—an equal part of God, the Great Intelligence dwells within *you*. No man or woman, however prominent or influential, possesses more. Can't you see then, the glorious opportunity, that we all have, to go forward together, with faith in each other, into the promised land of tomorrow? It was not intended that man should be idle, that he should be dependent upon his fellow man or that he should not have opportunity to give full expression to his developing talents and abilities. But the way man has been compelled to live, has made him, too often, lose sight of what he came into this life to accomplish. The struggle for existence has taken from man the time he has needed to get acquainted with his own self and to discover that he has a God-given power within him which can bring him a happiness of body and mind of which he has not dreamed.

Is a man necessarily happy because he slaves each day to earn enough money to buy food and clothes and shelter for his loved ones and himself? Is the rich man happy with his riches alone? Is a wife satisfied with the drudgery of housework? Are the duties of this world appealing in themselves? You know they are not—not a single one of them. They have to have a purpose behind them—some vital, understandable reason *why* a person is willing to put forth an effort and make sacrifices and strive to overcome obstacles.

You've got to feel that what you are doing is worthwhile— that it's really counting for something, that it's being appreciated by somebody, that you are playing a part with your fellow humans in making this world a better place in which to live. You may not put this purpose in so many words, but if you feel dissatisfied, and discouraged and can't see any future in what you are now doing, then you are out of step with your intended destiny in life and need to gain a deeper knowledge of yourself in order to discover your real place in the great scheme of things. I tell you positively that you have a place and no one can fill this place but you. So take a moment now to ask yourself if you have, as yet, found your real purpose in life.

Have you ever stopped to consider that you are where you are at this very moment because of what you are? Each new experience you've had in life has changed you, has done something to you, has given you a greater education, a greater wisdom, a greater understanding than you've ever had before whether you realize it or not. You may say, "But I'm worse off today than I was a few years or months ago." If you are, it's because you haven't made proper use of the experiences and opportunities you have had.

If you could only know it, your failures have been just as important to you as your successes. Your failures could have taught you how not to do things and what to do next time in order to attain success. But you may have been so upset by your failures that you regarded your time and effort spent as a total loss. Every man or woman who has gained any worthwhile success in life has had to learn to rise above failure and to use each failure as an added stepping stone to success.

When Dr. Ehrlich was finally able to give to the world his great cure for syphilis he called it "606" because he had failed 605 heartbreaking times before he succeeded in developing this preparation. And Thomas Edison made over *10,000* separate and distinct efforts before he found the right combination of elements which would make possible the electric light. No woman becomes a good cook the first time she boils water or bakes a cake. No man jumps overnight from office boy to the presidency of a company. No seed planted in the ground becomes a full grown tree the next morning.

The forces of nature and the forces of man require time for their unfoldment and development. You can hurry your own progress only by a more earnest application to the work at hand. There are no real short cuts. The man who spends his time getting promoted through pull and influence seldom is able to hold any important position for which he has not been fitted by experience. The person who reaches a goal through bluff and pretense can lose it just as quickly, once exposed.

You can't get something in this life for nothing—no matter how hard you try. It may seem so to you as you observe the lives of others. I've had friends say to me, "Look at So-and-So, he's always getting the breaks! And he doesn't do a thing to earn them." But these friends aren't in the best position to judge.

They can't be in this man's shoes. They can't possibly know what sacrifices he's made or what efforts he's put forth in order to get where he has. All they can observe is the goal he has reached. If he has arrived at his goal through anything but honest effort and the application of his talents and experience, then he won't last—he won't succeed unless those with whom he works carry the load for him. Unhappily there are many in this life carrying just such a load for others.

The people who really do succeed are people with a purpose. They know where they are going and why they are going there. They've either known it early in life or they've discovered through bitter experience and failure their real intended purpose and this discovery has led them on to the success which up to that time had eluded them. You can't really succeed in this life without a purpose. You can make money, get married, have friends, and do all the things that other people do in life but you'll always be restless, disappointed and dissatisfied unless behind everything you do is a consciousness of purpose.

If you would be a happy, contented and well-balanced person—physically, mentally and spiritually—life must mean something to you personally. It must have a reason behind it and you must be able to feel that you've gained something from life that can never be lost. Do you feel that way now? Can you honestly say, as you analyze yourself, that you've found your purpose in life? If you've not, then you can never be assured of lasting happiness until you do. Take this moment to give thought to what your purpose is or may be in life. If you know what your purpose is, then resolve to stand behind it with all the courage and energy and faith you possess.

The great need, today, for each and every one of us is to find our purpose. Without it we are as aimless in our journey on the sea of life as a ship without a rudder. We have nothing to steer us or guide us.

Why do so many people go to pieces physically and mentally when they suffer financial loss? Because such men and women have established no real values beyond those represented by the almighty dollar. Life has had no meaning to them without it, and they have seen no purpose in trying to go on living. Without money they were helpless, practically paralyzed in body and in spirit. And yet the greatest, most wonderful forces of life were still about them, ready to respond to their bidding the instant they gained a new sense of values and came to realize the purpose for their existence.

You see—you came into this world to serve your fellow man and to be served by him. You can't get away from this responsibility. You couldn't continue to live without the daily toil of thousands of men and women whom you will never see. But what you are doing, as unimportant as it may seem to you, must mean something to someone else. The more civilized we have grown the more dependent we actually have become upon one another. This is an age of special skills and talents. Few of us can do more than one thing exceedingly well. But what we can do well we give in exchange to others who can return to us the services we are incapable of performing for ourselves.

Can you now begin to see the great pattern behind all life? Can you begin to sense the great scheme of things? You are as indispensable and as vitally needed to this scheme as anyone else. If you fail in your part, in your purpose—then the contribution you were intended to make during your lifetime here will be forever lost. No one just like you, with just your qualifications has ever lived before—and there will be no one ever again with just your possibilities.

You may not have been born with the physical and mental endowments of someone else, but you do possess an absolutely equal portion of this God-given creative power within your own mind. No human being—and no force on earth—can take this power from you. It is yours to call upon as you wish and if you know your real purpose in life then you are in complete harmony with the working of this God-given power and you are certain to reach your goal and render your intended service.

Right now—this minute—whoever you are, wherever you are, you can call upon this God-given power within you by an effort of your will. Deep down within you, if you will think as you are reading these lines, you'll know what you should have been doing with your life if you are not. Your real inner self knows what you came here with the opportunity of doing. It knows whether you've failed thus far in accomplishing it. It knows whether you've allowed yourself to become sidetracked on one of life's many byways and whether you've passed up the opportunities which have been given you to make the most of your life.

Yes, this part of God, the Great Intelligence, which dwells within you, knows all these things. But you have been created a creature of *free will.* You will never be compelled to fulfill your intended destiny in life. This has been left to you as a matter of your free choice.

If you feel now that you have failed in whole or in part—if you feel that you've not lived up to the best that's within you, don't waste any time feeling bad over the past but find your purpose now and look ahead to the goal which can still be yours. This goal may never win you any earthly recognition or reward; this goal may not bring you any plaudits of the crowd or financial gain or even human appreciation—but for you to have realized in your own mind and heart that you have a purpose to fulfill—that you have a rendezvous with your own destiny and that this calls for your doing the best you can in whatever situation you find yourself, no matter how great the obstacle or trying the circumstance, is for you to have lived your life triumphantly and well.

Your purpose, then, is to meet life the best you can, each step of the way, in the knowledge and faith that all things of this world can be taken from you, but you still have lost nothing because you are at peace with your real self. You know

now, at last, the truth of that old saying, "Greater is he who gaineth his own soul, than he who taketh a city."

There's a new day dawning. Perhaps from your hilltop in life you cannot see this new day as yet. Perhaps you are still in the valley of fear and despair. Perhaps you've been enshrouded by the dark mantle of grief. Perhaps it seems to you that you can never know joy again. But even in the midst of these terrible world conditions I believe in this new day.

This day is dawning, first in the hearts and minds of men—in your heart and my heart, in your mind and my mind. There's a complete change coming—a change in man's attitude toward his fellow man. We are all going to know, beyond a shadow of doubt, why we are here together on this earth and what our individual and common purposes are. We're going to see clearly, for the first time, what we need to do to work together with peoples of different nations but of the same human family. We're going to see that since we each possess an equal part of God, the Great Intelligence, within, none of us should be favored over another. We're going to realize that only by giving this God-power within us a free and unlimited opportunity for expression can we gain the happiness in life we seek.

This God-power has been with us throughout our entire lives but we haven't begun to make full or intelligent use of it. If we had, World Wars I and II couldn't have been—nor the other great wars of history. We have preferred to rely upon our animal natures, our own emotions and material desires, to get for us what we've thought we wanted. But, after we've gotten it—wealth, position, worldly power—we then know that it still doesn't mean anything, that something deeply satisfying is missing, that until we feel that we've become united with something higher and finer within our own selves, and have found our real place in the scheme of things, nothing else we've accomplished matters.

Are you happy with wealth or without it? Is it because you possess wealth or because you lack wealth that you are unhappy?

In this new day that is dawning you're going to be compelled to give up many things upon which you've placed high value but you're going to possess other things of real and lasting value—the love and understanding of your fellow man. This one development alone is going to change the face of the earth and all things upon it. Those of you who fail to recognize this fact and insist on clinging to the old order of class distinction and race prejudice and creedal difference and various kinds of hates and fears are going to find yourselves out of step and unable to keep pace with the new marching song of a united humanity.

There's a time of trouble and possible discord still ahead, but I can hear the strains of a new harmony breaking through. That is why I am urging you to gain the right to live your own life and then to find, at all costs, your real purpose in life. Once you do this you'll be ready to take your part in the world of tomorrow.

I suggest to you now, that you set aside a time, each day, preferably in the evening after your day's work is done, to sit quietly and look ahead, with confidence and faith in the future. Ask yourself each night if you've done everything humanly possible to further your purpose. Ask of this God-power within that you be given increasing knowledge and wisdom. Picture yourself being a better husband or wife, a better mother or father to your children, a better daughter or son to your parents, a better friend to all who give you their friendship, and a better person in every way.

If you will do this, your purpose in life will reveal itself to you. Each thought and act will take on new meaning and you will feel yourself unmistakably a part of the great plan for human betterment which is unfolding on this earth.

One of our great troubles in the world of today is the fact that we developed so fast mechanically and scientifically, we couldn't keep pace mentally and spiritually. We didn't know how to use our mechanical and scientific marvels for our own good. We lost sight of the purpose behind these great inventions, which came through the minds of men as a result of the workings of this great God-given power within them.

These wonderful advances in science and industry were intended to free us all, not to enslave us, physically and economically; to free us so that we might find our real purpose in life and go forward together—all races, colors and creeds—toward a single great goal of human achievement: Universal Brotherhood. But somehow, because the lower side of us is still close to animal, we got lost along the way. Somehow, our greeds and hates and prejudices and fears and distrust of our fellow man came in like a hurricane to destroy these higher and finer ambitions within us and bring upon the world this present chaos. All this time God, the Great Intelligence, has not deserted us but we have deserted Him.

This God-power is just as much a part of us now as it has always been. But remember, we've been created creatures of free will and free choice. We'll never be compelled to draw upon this God-power. We must do it of our free will. And when we do, we lift ourselves immediately above the animal in us to this higher self—this part of God, the Great Intelligence—and then we know, perhaps for the first time, that we really are more than animal . . . that there's something in us which is eternal, something that is going to survive what we call death, something that knows it is here for a purpose, and *that* something is your own self—your own soul.

There's so much to tell you about yourself and I desire to make it as clear to you as I possibly can. But I do not wish you to accept these statements of mine on faith alone. I want you to take them with an open mind and prove them out in your own life. It would be very difficult to prove to an African native that the air was full of sounds he could not hear unless you had a radio set with you and could turn it on and take these sounds out of the air. But all I'm telling you I've proved to my satisfaction in my own life. And you must prove these same truths for yourself.

Once you are convinced beyond all doubt that this God-power dwells within you, you'll develop a courage and a faith you never dreamed possible. You'll be able to face any condition in life, no matter how difficult, with a calmness and a poise and a confidence of overcoming it. This is what I promise you who will sincerely strive to understand yourself and to follow your real purpose in life.

How can you accomplish your purpose in life? It can't be done by wearing yourself out physically and mentally with fears and worries and all the destructive emotions such as greed and hate. You see, your real self knows why you are here and what you are supposed to do with your life. But if you get mixed up with all your physical desires and fears and worries and haven't learned how to control them, then you're very apt to lose sight of your goal and live a restless, aimless, unsatisfactory, disappointed life.

You can easily recognize the man or woman with a purpose. There's something magnetic and appealing about them which sets them apart. This is because these people have been knowingly using each experience which comes to them as a foundation stone in their life of purpose and they are expressing this purpose in everything they do.

A person may have a fine singing voice and be technically perfect in the rendition of every song, but unless he has lived and expresses understanding and genuine feeling in his singing, he'll never touch a responsive chord in his listeners. Madame Schumann-Heink, who had two sons on each side of the first World War, took a little German folk song, "Silent Night, Holy Night," and breathed into it her own mother-love, and touched the heart of all humanity.

Yehudi Menuhin, one of the world's greatest violinists, is noted for the generous giving-out of his rare talent. A few years ago, in a summer concert at Lewisohn Stadium in New York, Mr. Menuhin remained playing encores long after the orchestra had left and the lights had been turned out. He played on under the stars, as his listeners joined their souls with his and felt, through the medium of music, a kinship with the finest things in life.

Purpose means everything to each one of us, young or old. It's fine to have a book education, but unless it can be applied to life and living and the betterment of mankind, a person can be trapped by his own intellectual attainments and lose the very thing he's seeking. It's great to become a doctor but all the letters in the alphabet after his name will mean nothing until through his knowledge he saves a life. There's no nobler profession on earth than motherhood but a mother has not attained her real purpose until she has trained her children to take their places in the world and has given them to the world.

You'll find once your life is dominated by your purpose that you'll want to give freely and joyously of your talents and services because you'll know that they don't belong to you alone and should not selfishly be withheld from the world. All of the planet's great spiritual leaders, inspired as they've been by their high purpose, have recognized this great universal truth, "It is more blessed to give than to receive." When you begin giving yourself, in keeping with your own purpose in life, you'll commence growing and developing and you'll know in your mind and heart that you've found your place in life, and that the world itself is better for your having lived!

Your life is just what you make it by your thinking. The successful man or woman pictures success and puts forth every effort to help bring this success to pass. No man can really succeed who lacks faith in himself. This creative power, within your mind, can't work for you unless you have this faith. Your fears destroy this faith. They keep you from thinking right and acting right. If what you want in life has not come to you, it's up to you to eliminate all fear thoughts.

I know that you, who read these words, may be living a life of fear and worry. You can't bear the thought of being alone, or going out on the street by yourself. You're afraid you may be losing your mind or that evil influences are surrounding you. Behind all this is, perhaps, a terrorizing fear of death.

And, I say to you who fear, *that you are never alone*—that a part of God, the Great Intelligence, dwells within you—*that you* only have to learn how to call upon this great and unlimited God-power in order to be guided and protected.

Remember—this power is supposed to be your servant. It's supposed to take orders from you in the form of the mental pictures you give it of what you wish to be or do. And if your mental pictures are right—if your thinking is correct—what happens to you will be right!

You can't possibly fear once you've come really to know and feel the presence of God-within you! There isn't a force on earth—a man or woman or circumstance of any kind—that can really hurt or affect you so long as you place your faith in this God-power—and exercise your *will* to think the right thoughts. Once you do your part, God will do His.

But you must do your part first and, when you do, you'll find a new strength and courage sufficient to meet every situation in life. Faith in yourself and faith in God are the key to mastery of fear.

Fear cannot remain in the presence of faith. I give you now something to repeat each morning as you awaken and each night as you drop off to sleep: "Fear knocked at the door, faith opened it, and there was nothing there."

Courage, then, to face and solve your life problems as you should. Your Key to Happiness is knowledge of self and I now present to you, in the pages to come, this Key! But you must open the door to this new understanding, yourself. Do not read this book—*study* it! Start practicing right thinking from this moment on, and good things will commence happening to you. It won't be long before you'll be joining the chorus of increasing thousands of men and women who are joyously testifying "It works!"

CHAPTER ONE

The Key to Your Inner Self

Would you like to meet the most interesting person in the world to you? Would you like to know the only person who has the power to bring you happiness, health and the things in life you desire above all else? I know you would and so I am going to introduce you to that person. That person is *yourself.*

Does that startle or amaze you? If it does, then it will surprise you more when I say that I doubt if you have, as yet, met your real self. I think you will readily agree that this is so when I have finished introducing you to yourself.

It may seem strange that I, who have never met you, should presume to know so much about you. The fact actually is that there is no basic difference between us. That is because *your* mind and *my* mind—and the minds of all humans—operate in accordance with a certain great mental law. And I have only to understand the nature of this law to know *you*—yes, even the problems that are facing you!

Things may have been going wrong with you for some time. You may be under great economic pressure. You may have had your courage and faith in life severely tested. You may have had a falling out with a best friend or a disagreement with your husband or wife, as the case may be. You may feel that you have failed in your duties as a parent or as a mate, that the future holds very little promise of happiness or health or financial relief for you. You may be wondering, at this very moment, whether there is any real way out of the difficulties that surround you. And, if you are, my answer to you is, "Don't lose hope! There is a way to solve your problems, to relieve the conditions which may now be pressing in upon you—a way that will enable you to achieve the things in life which mean most to you."

If you want more money, this way will bring it to you. This power within yourself, which I am about to reveal to you, is like an Aladdin's lamp. It produces for you whatever you wish, once you know how to command its hidden, almost magic force. Should you desire to be a painter or a musician, providing you possess undeveloped talent along these lines, this power will liberate your talent and attract to you the circumstances and means by which you can achieve success as a painter or musician.

It makes no difference what success you would like to attain—whether it be success in love, success in marriage, success in overcoming obstacles, or success in arriving at any one of a hundred different objectives. The power of which I speak can bring you that success dependent only upon the ability you develop for drawing upon this power and directing it for your own good.

And the way to develop this ability is for you to be able to *picture* clearly in your mind whatever success you desire. You may not realize it but everything that has happened to you, up to this present moment, has come about because you first saw it happening in your mind's eye. You can look back upon the many plans you have made; how earnestly and vividly you *pictured* doing them; and how, step by step, as you kept the same vision in your mind, your plans were perfected in actual life. But they had existed, first, only in your mind!

You've often heard people say, "I was afraid that would happen!" The chances are you've made this statement many times yourself. And yet, you've probably overlooked the fact that you had, through fear, mentally pictured certain things occurring and they had come to pass!

This creative power within you has no reasoning faculty. It cannot recognize the difference between the good and the bad. If you picture success, this power brings it. Picture failure, you will have it.

And that is why it is so necessary for you to know how to control this power, how to control the nature of your thought pictures so that you will not cause this power to bring you grief instead of happiness. Learning how to do this is so simple and understandable that you can, as soon as the inner working of your mind is explained, begin mentally picturing the things you desire; this will put you on the road toward solving any present difficulties, lifting you from where you are to where you wish to be.

But before you can accomplish this, there are a few facts about yourself that you must know. You must know, for instance, that you actually have two separate and distinct minds. There is your *Conscious* mind which deals with the world you live in. Then there is your inner or *Subconscious* mind which deals with the vast, uncharted world within yourself; a world that Science, with all its knowledge, knows very little about.

You use your Conscious mind to do your reasoning, doubting, guessing, wondering, calculating and assimilating. It is like a sieve that lets everything soak through it, after filtering out what isn't wanted. But everything upon which you center the attention of your Conscious mind is recorded in the form of a *mental picture* and passed on to your inner mind, the Subconscious, where it is filed away for future reference. And, while you may not realize it, your Conscious mind has no creative power. Its power ends with its ability to hand over to your Subconscious its reactions and thoughts on matters of interest to you.

Your inner or Subconscious mind, however, possesses unlimited creative power. It cannot reason, as I have said, since your reasoning faculty is a function of your Conscious mind. Therefore, if your Conscious mind has not guarded you against a wrong mental picture—and has passed it on to your Subconscious—your inner mind isn't going to stop to question the ill-effect that the reproduction of this wrong mental picture may have upon you in your actual life. It is going to turn its creative power upon that mental picture and bring it into being. And the only way to keep your Subconscious mind from following the wrong mental pictures is to substitute the *right* kind of mental pictures before it has a chance to go to work on the bad ones.

Let me prove to you that your Conscious mind has no creative power and that it is your Subconscious mind which really produces all ideas and solutions for you.

Remember the times when you tried and tried to solve an important question in your life? You walked the floor. You did everything but tear your hair. And finally, despairing of a solution, you sat down, almost exhausted, and said, "I give up. I simply can't figure it out!"

Yet, strangely enough, as soon as you did give up, the answer flashed into your mind and you cried out, "I have it! Now I know what to do!" That solution came about with no *conscious* thinking on your part at all. It apparently shot into your mind like a bolt from the blue. But it was not an accident. In trying to solve that problem you had, without knowing it, commanded your Subconscious mind to create the solution for you. You gave it all the facts you had, in the form of mental pictures. But you held your Conscious mind, which had no power to create an answer, too tense—you tied it in a knot—and, consequently, your Subconscious mind couldn't make itself heard. The minute you relaxed, however, it immediately slipped the answer into your Conscious mind.

When you have learned to see your mind at work, you will be able to look back over your life and see for yourself how your own wrong mental pictures have attracted wrong conditions to you. You will then be convinced that everything that has happened in this external world in which we live, has first taken place in someone's mind. There is nothing mysterious or supernatural about it. It is all in accordance with the infallible working out of an existent mental law which humans, from the beginning of time, have unknowingly operated either for their own good or ill.

To aid you in achieving that which you desire, I am going to give you a formula for reaching and controlling your Subconscious mind at any time you wish. This formula, properly understood and put into operation, will enable you to picture mentally the things you really want. Having pictured these things you will, in due course of time, have the thrill of seeing them actually come to pass, brought into being through the infallible working out of this Universal Law.

Here is the formula:

First: Relax your body.

Second: Free your Conscious mind of all conflicting thoughts.

Third: With your body relaxed and your Conscious mind at ease, fix your attention on a mental picture of what you want to achieve.

That means *concentrate!* Form an exact mental picture of what you desire to attain in life. See it in your mind's eye. Visualize the things you want as coming to you or happening to you. Picture it so vividly that you can see yourself *doing* it or *being* it or *having* it.

As you increase your ability to picture vividly what you want, it will come closer and closer to you. Finally, you will find what you have desired, right there at your command.

Thomas Edison, the world's greatest inventor, to whom we are indebted for the phonograph, the motion picture and the electric light, used this formula which I have given you in achieving his marvelous inventions. When he was asked one day how he accounted for his amazing inventive genius, Mr. Edison smiled and said, "It is because I never think in words; I think in pictures." He saw a picture in his mind's eye of the object he desired to invent and his Subconscious mind then started to work on it. As he kept this picture of the object before him, he got creative hunches and, step by step, he followed the line of experimenting which occurred to him until there came a day when the invention he had visualized was an actual accomplishment.

Every one who has achieved anything worthwhile in life has consciously or unconsciously made use of this formula— this law of the Subconscious mind—which has been given you. The same power which served Thomas Edison exists within you, ready to serve you to the degree that you are able to command it.

Recently, in a Middle Western town, the death of "Cheerful Tom" was reported. His death was grieved by the population of the entire city and yet few of Tom's fellow townsmen had ever seen him. But, despite this, he was as well known as the mayor. There was hardly a man or woman who had not heard his cheery voice on the telephone and few, who were in the market for magazines, that had not given him their subscription.

Tom, shortly following his marriage, had suffered an accident that crushed both his legs and injured his spine. The accident doomed him to be bedridden the remainder of his life. But was Tom downhearted? Did he permit this catastrophe to warp his future, to blight his happiness and that of the girl who had married him? Did he visualize himself as a helpless invalid, one who must be cared for perhaps by an institution, or else supported by relatives? Hardly!

Tom had no sooner been confronted with the facts concerning his condition than he dried the tears of his wife with a resolution and a spirit that would have shamed many an able-bodied man.

Then, setting about to reconstruct his world and adapt himself to an entirely new type of environment, Tom hit upon the idea of soliciting magazine subscriptions by telephone. His voice possessed personality and appeal. People listened and placed their orders. They told friends; friends asked Tom's phone number; Tom became better and better acquainted with families throughout the town. He worked eight hours a day propped up in bed. His gay laugh and witty tongue brought moments of relaxation to weary housewives who were never too tired to chat with him. He soon came to know a great deal about human psychology through telephone conversations. Money came rolling in, enough to hire a permanent secretary, enough to buy Tom's wife the little luxuries that a woman craves; enough to bring Tom all the ease his condition permitted.

And when Cheerful Tom passed on, at an advanced age, there were sad hearts in many a home. His voice had "died" to them; they missed the sound of his cheery personality on the wire. In death, almost the whole town passed in review to see the crippled body which had housed an unconquerable soul. Tom had turned possible defeat into magnificent triumph; he had proven stronger in adversity than he had proved in command of all his physical faculties. He had left his stamp in the hearts and minds of a populace that might not otherwise have known he existed.

This was all due to Tom's mental picturing and rebuilding his life through visualization—seeing himself becoming a success and achieving happiness despite what might have seemed to many an insurmountable handicap.

You may, at this very moment, be injuring your health or bringing about a succession of unhappy circumstances by permitting the flow of worry and fear thoughts and picturing dire consequences occurring to yourself. Therefore, I urge you to erase at once such mental pictures from the inner screen of your Subconscious mind.

To do this: remember first to relax your body, then free your Conscious mind of all conflicting thoughts, and finally, with your body relaxed and your mind at ease, fix your entire attention on what you want to achieve. See it in your mind's eye. See it as though it were on a motion picture screen, as an actual movie in operation. Happening to *you*, the things you desire coming *to* you.

Much can be accomplished in a short time. Start now visualizing mental pictures for increased health, happiness and the other good things of life. As you grow in understanding of yourself, the results you attain will thrill and amaze you. They are dependent only upon your ability to visualize them!

(a) **Relaxation**

Do you ever get tired?

This question, I realize, is utterly ridiculous. But here is a series of questions not half so absurd:

When you get tired, what do you do about it? Do you know how to relax completely? Do you know how to quiet and soothe throbbing nerves? Do you know how to revitalize your physical being naturally and to restore your normal healthy and happy spirit?

If you do, you are one of the few in every ten thousand who have learned, knowingly or unknowingly, how to call upon the resources of your Subconscious mind.

When I tell you now of how to relax your physical body completely, you are going to be amazed at certain discoveries you will make. You have never realized before what a hold your Conscious mind has upon your body, how definitely each thought is affecting different nerve centers and how—even as you are reading these very words—your Conscious mind is aware of everything that is physically happening to you. Let me prove it to you.

As you are reading this, let your thoughts turn to your body and immediately you will be conscious of a slightly cramped position. If your knees are crossed, it may be the pressure of one leg against another. You may be suddenly conscious of an elbow resting on the arm of your chair. A portion of your face may want to be rubbed for no good reason at all. Of these, and a hundred and one other little sensations, your Conscious mind is constantly aware.

And so, the first step necessary toward the complete relaxation of your body, is to *free* your body of your Conscious mind. This may seem, at the moment, an impossibility until I remind you that you actually free your body of your Conscious mind every night when you drop to sleep. This time, however, you will learn to withdraw your Conscious mind from your body without dropping off to sleep! The instant you are able to do this, you will experience a sensation of physical relief and exhilaration that is beyond anything you have imagined.

I presume you are seated in a chair. But, no matter what your position, lying or sitting, make yourself physically as comfortable as possible. You are about to do some mental picturing to put this formula to the test-to see for yourself how simply and marvelously it works!

First, direct the attention of your Conscious mind to your feet and legs. Visualize your Conscious mind now as leaving your legs. Your Conscious mind is traveling up your body, letting go its hold of different portions of your body as it travels, having an increasingly calming and quieting effect upon your nerves. Lift an arm and let it drop as though it no longer belongs to you. Do the same with the other arm. Now, as your Conscious mind reaches your head, having released its hold upon the rest of your physical being, you have commenced to feel a lightness and a restfulness that you probably never sensed before. If this has been the first time you have ever *consciously* withdrawn your Conscious mind from your body, the relief brought by true relaxation may make you feel as if you could drop off to sleep.

But now that you have physically relaxed and your Conscious mind has been removed from the body, you are ready to use your Will Control to place the mental picture of that which you desire in your life upon what I call the "motion picture screen" of your inner or Subconscious mind. You are ready, in other words, to *concentrate*, to *see*, in your mind's eye, a confident, vivid picture of yourself *doing* something or *being* something or *having* something worthwhile.

A woman friend of mine, who knows how to relax and how to picture what she desires, has the reputation of being "always on the go"; possessing a seemingly inexhaustible supply of energy which enables her to supervise her housework, care for her three children and still find time for her clubs, church work and civic activities. She has told me that she owes her many accomplishments to the discovery that she can gain the equivalent of some hours' sleep by ten to twenty minutes of complete relaxation. After a strenuous morning of housework, with a bridge party scheduled for the afternoon and a social engagement at night, she sees to it that she has ten to twenty minutes at different intervals of the day, in which to get off by herself and sit in a chair or stretch out upon a bed. She then "lets go" as she says, clearing her mind of all body impressions of weariness, relaxing the tightened, jumpy nerves and mentally picturing herself in a state of renewed vigor.

Many wives are so tired and worn by nightfall that they are not agreeable companions for their husbands. Nerves that are on edge cause the nerves of others to react wrongly and much needless unhappiness is brought about because humans have not learned to relax and to take life less seriously.

A husband may also be at fault for the same reason: too much high pressure at the office. Perhaps he hasn't a job at present, and too strenuous activity or a trying, period of inactivity causes severe nerve strain, digestive disturbances and other physical upsets; these serving in turn to destroy a husband's good humor and the consideration he should show for the woman he loves.

Every man and woman needs the knowledge of how to relax as a means of throwing off the tension of present day living. Try this way of relaxing. Each time you repeat it, you will notice more beneficial results.

(b) Concentration

You have heard, perhaps, that it requires months and years to learn how to concentrate. You probably have thought, if you were denied certain educational advantages, that it wasn't much use trying to improve your mind and, consequently, you would have to get along as best you could with such a mind as you have.

If you have had any such thoughts, put them out of your mind forever. You possess as good a mind as any person on earth, if you will only learn how to make use of it. A schooling or college education is a fine thing but, if circumstances have denied much learning to you, you can still attain success in life through applying your mind properly. Some of the world's greatest geniuses were self-educated men and women, who visualized success for themselves, who saw themselves overcoming all handicaps, who gained the heights first through achieving a thorough knowledge of their inner resources and how and when to draw upon them.

Your inner mind does not require a college education to function for you. It does not require even a grade school education. But it *does* require an ability on your part to visualize vivid pictures for it. And all you have to do, to produce these pictures successfully is to relax your physical body so that you are at ease; so that your Conscious mind is not disturbed by any physical impressions of discomfort. Then, with your Conscious mind also at ease, in a passive state, you have only to exert your Will to call forth the mental picture of that thing you desire. And this mental picture must be seen clearly on what I call the "motion picture screen" of your inner mind.

In order to see a clear mental picture of that which you desire, you must learn how to "blank" your mind. By blanking your mind I mean having the ability, at will, to eliminate the flow of worry and fear thoughts which ordinarily run constantly back and forth across your inner consciousness. The moment you have learned how to blot out all conscious thoughts—to make your Conscious mind passive—you will be able to concentrate.

And here is a method by which you can attain the ability to concentrate at once. This method will enable you to hold *one* thought in your mind and to keep out every other thought or mental picture. This is all that concentration is: focusing your attention on one thought to the exclusion of all others. As you are reading this, with your eyes wide open, turn your thoughts inward and see, in your imagination, a white motion picture screen stretched across your inner field of consciousness. Imagine yourself in a motion picture theater, perfectly relaxed and gazing at the screen before any picture has been thrown upon it; only, this time, the motion picture screen is in your mind's eye.

While you are reading this, you now *see* or *feel* this white motion picture screen. It is there, waiting for you to throw whatever picture you want upon it—just as though you, yourself, are the motion picture projection machine. You can hold this screen blank for so long as you desire—you *have* been holding it blank as you have been reading this—and now you are going to throw a picture on this screen, in which you see yourself *doing* or *being* or *having* something that you very much desire.

See this mental motion picture of yourself as though what you are doing or being or having has already happened! *Know* that you are capable and deserving of that which you are seeing *already* accomplished. And once you have clearly seen or felt this picture, forget about it. Let the curtain fall upon your motion picture screen. You have now closed the shutter upon your camera. The picture is impressed upon your Subconscious mind and your inner mind will immediately set to work to develop it in your external life.

Bit by bit, as you visualize this same picture day after day, you will see parts of your picture reproduced in your actual life. You may meet a new person who will supply something you need to make your vision come true. You may apparently run into certain information which will aid you in arriving at your goal. You may find certain friends or relatives commencing to take a different attitude toward you. Whatever your mental picture, you may expect it all to come to pass if you have visualized every portion of your picture vividly and confidently enough; but if only a *part* of your picture works out, get busy on the angles that have not materialized. Do some more concentrating on these angles; and be ready and willing to put forth every physical effort to help your Subconscious mind in the hunches it will give you and the opportunities that will bob up which will lead to the actual completion of your mental picture.

Practice this method of concentration daily until you have mastered the art of relaxation and acquired the ability to visualize the things in life you desire. You are dealing with an inner power that, rightly used, can liberate you from unhappy, intolerable conditions; a power which, universally employed, could cure most of the ills of the world!

CHAPTER TWO

The Creative Power Within You

Many of you who are reading this book will realize that you have been making use of this great mental law for years; that, while you were without any conscious technique for operating the law, you were getting results just the same. And now, of course, you are thrilled and happy to have a formula by which you can *consciously* control your inner mind and greatly increase your percentage of successful achievement.

No one knows what is possible to the mind of man. We have seen apparent miracles accomplished in sport, in business, in all walks of life. We have seen mental giants like the electrical wizard, Steinmetz, whose great mind overcame the handicap of a crippled body. We have seen women like Helen Keller who, though deaf, dumb and blind, developed the power of expression—a personality, an intelligence and a fortitude against apparent hopeless odds that should forever shame any of us who think we are overwhelmed with handicaps, that life has given us no chance.

Your mind can liberate you from any predicament or set of obstacles if you will only let it; if you will learn how to release certain great creative forces within you which you have either been misdirecting or have not called upon. Now is the time to picture the happiness, health and success which should be yours. Others are doing it and getting marvelous results. And what they are doing, as I have reiterated, you also can do!

You mustn't be impatient or over-anxious because this will destroy the value of your mental picturing. You can't get your Subconscious mind to work for you by using force thoughts. You must always be completely relaxed and, without the slightest doubt, *see* the things coming to you that you most desire. You must be able to feel that you have earned the right to these things you desire ; that you deserve to have them— or that you are willing to make the effort necessary for their achievement. If this is your mental attitude toward the things you picture, your Subconscious mind will see to it that you attain them, that circumstances are attracted to you which will enable you to realize your objective in life.

You ask how the Subconscious does these seeming miracles. I answer that it possesses a creative power which can be demonstrated under *conscious* control, just as we can witness the power of electricity without knowing basically what electricity really is. We know enough about electricity, however, to use it to our very great advantage; and the same is true of our Subconscious mind. We are beginning to understand how it functions. We have discovered that it has the faculty of reproducing in our outer world, the things we have pictured for it. We have come to realize that all the great inventions—the radio, the telephone, the airplane, the automobile, television and countless other mechanical marvels—were first created for us by this power within us. These marvels first existed in the *mind* of man before they became realities! And this gives us the assurance that many more wonders are contained within the consciousness of each one of us if we can only develop the faculty to bring them to the surface.

Remember—you must see yourself as having *already* attained a certain objective in life. It is like a cake that has been baked. This cake contains all the ingredients, in another form, which were first mixed into it. So it is with your objective but, in the case of your objective, your Conscious mind can't possibly know all the ingredients that are required in the actual reproducing of it. However, your Subconscious mind knows instinctively and intuitively what is required and you should leave to it this part of the task.

Be sure that you thoroughly understand this fact: it is not necessary to picture each step of the way to attain the thing you desire. The Subconscious mind will work out the steps for you, much better and more surely than you can possibly do it since your own Conscious mind is limited in operation. It is bounded by the five senses while your Subconscious mind has no consciousness of time or space, being behind everything that you have done or are doing.

Set a regular time each day for visualizing what you want. At first you will need practice to see pictures on the screen of your inner mind or to feel intensely that a certain thing is coming to pass. Continued practice, however, will create a new freedom of body, mind and spirit that cannot now be imagined.

(*a*) **Importance of Right Mental Pictures**

A few years ago I met an elderly woman who said to me, "Mr. Sherman, all my life I've feared poverty, pictured the horror of it in old age, saw it and fought against it. To prevent it coming to me, I saved, invested and amassed a modest fortune. But now I have lost everything. The Wall Street crash and a bank failure have ruined me. What I've feared has come. Here I am, old and almost penniless. What shall I do?"

When I told this woman how, by picturing poverty so vividly, by fearing it for herself she had finally achieved it in spite of all her saving and investing, she was dumfounded. "But," she replied, "What can I do now, at my age? There's nothing left for me but the poorhouse!"

"There you go again!" I pointed out to her. "You are not content with having achieved poverty; now you want the poorhouse. Let me tell you, if you picture the poorhouse, you'll get the poorhouse! Your inner mind has no reasoning power. It takes whatever mental pictures you give it and works them out, whether they are designed for your good or bad. Since you have no money, why not picture yourself as the life companion of a woman *with* money? There are many charming elderly women of means who are lonely and in need of the companionship you could afford them. If you could see yourself in such a position, it would not be long until such an opportunity is attracted to you!"

"That's an idea!" this woman exclaimed, with renewed hope. "I'll try it!"

Several months later, her continued mental picturing resulted in her being employed by a wealthy woman as companion on a world tour. She had entirely erased the fear of poverty from her mind and poverty, as a result, could not exist any longer in her actual life.

I know you are anxious to get results through visualizing the things in life you want but be sure you do not attempt to *force* these things to happen. You should be so confident that you deserve the things you desire or so willing to put forth the effort necessary to earn whatever you wish to, achieve that you are able to maintain a completely relaxed attitude.

You will know, inwardly, whether you are mentally trying to force a condition to come to pass. You will feel a tenseness in your body and a tenseness in your mind; and the instant you feel this way, let go. Sit back and analyze why you feel as you do. It indicates there is a weak link somewhere in your visualizing. You are actually afraid that you lack the ability to bring the thing you are mentally picturing to you and, as a substitute for this ability, you have permitted the forcing element to creep in. And yet, nothing basically worth while or lasting has ever been achieved by force since the world began.

Whatever is achieved by force can always be destroyed by force. That which is not really earned can be taken away. If you gain by trying to compel others to obey or conform to your mental picturing of a situation, you lay yourself open to being used by others who have designs upon you. Like attracts like. What you give out, comes back to you, gathering power on the way.

A businessman who had dealt unfairly and unethically for years, taking advantage of others, suddenly realized that his wrong thinking and acting had begun to punish him severely. He came to me and asked me this question: "Mr. Sherman— tell me, please, what mental law can I operate to prevent others from doing to me what I have done to them?"

I was glad to answer that such a mental law does not exist. We all pay the penalty for wrong thinking sooner or later. The only protection possible to us is in changing drastically our own misdirected consciousness, rebuilding our thought structure so as to make it incapable of repeating past wrongs against ourselves and others.

Merely declaring our good intentions and asking others to forgive us does not release us from our debt to the chain of unfortunate circumstances we may have created. We must prove, by our present actions, the genuineness of our new mental attitude before we can liberate ourselves from the hold that we have permitted unhappy external conditions to gain over us.

Defeats you have suffered in life, inferiorities you may have developed and physical handicaps, either real or imaginary, may be keeping you from visualizing the things in life you desire. You will have to go to work on these complexes, mentally picturing yourself the master of them in order to free your mind from their domination.

At first, as you have practiced visualizing—seeing pictures of yourself achieving things in your mind's eye—you have probably noticed that it has been easier for you to implant wrong pictures upon your "motion picture screen" than right ones!

This is due to the fact that you have probably not learned emotional control. Few persons have. And your emotions, uncontrolled, can dictate a mental picture that you have no desire to see reproduced in your outer world. For instance, fear of a certain thing coming to pass may be made stronger, by your emotional reaction to it, than the very opposite which you would like to see happen. And yet, since your Subconscious has no reasoning power, you will be made the victim of your fear emotion unless you can, through using your Conscious Will control, present your inner mind with a clear, strong picture, offsetting the wrong one.

Say to yourself: "It is ridiculous for me to fear this thing. It is powerless to do me any harm and I have complete command over it!" You must be able to believe this—not merely say it for the sake of repeating the words—although a simple declaration will often give you courage and lend strength to your visualization.

Let us consider yourself as you are at the present moment, the associations that are yours, your position and circumstances in life. You have just gained a working knowledge of the formula for reaching and controlling your Subconscious mind at will and are eager to put it in operation. But, if you have tried it, you are almost certain to have encountered some of the emotional and mental obstacles I have mentioned. You, perhaps, have also made the mistake of visualizing friends and acquaintances doing things for you: recognizing your ability, helping your advancement in a personal or business way. As one woman said to me, "It's a form of mesmerism, isn't it? If I can just broadcast my thoughts into the minds of friends or those who are in position to do me some good, and give them the impulse to help me, that's all that's necessary!"

No, that's *not* all that's necessary. It's the wrong mental attitude to take in visualizing. It was intended that we humans should be creatures of free choice and free will. Most of the troubles of this world have already been caused because we have tried to impose our ideas and our desires upon others. And there is a mental law that protects you from the "force" or "desire" thoughts of others. Your Subconscious is constantly repulsing untold numbers of "force" thoughts that have been discharged into this sea of universal consciousness in something like the manner that radio waves are constantly being discharged into the ether.

Your mental attitude in picturing objectives you wish to attain should be a highly personalized feeling with regard to yourself and an absolutely impersonal feeling where others in your mental picture are concerned. This attitude will protect you from consciously or unconsciously assuming any "force" thoughts in connection with them. If others must occupy your picture, let your attitude toward them be one of detachment. You would like them in your picture when it has become a reality if it is right for them to be there and in accordance with their own desires, not yours.

No two humans have the same desires or are ready for and equal to the same conditions at the same time. Each life must be lived and experienced separately, however seemingly in association with others.

If you are looking for employment, visualize yourself occupying the position you desire. Do not picture yourself getting it through any particular place or one of several persons. See yourself already in possession of the job. See clearly the qualifications you have for that job. See, in your mind's eye, an unidentified individual or firm recognizing the worth of these qualifications. Tell yourself, with confidence, that someone at this very moment is visualizing, consciously or unconsciously, a *need* for just such work or services as you are equipped to render. See yourself being attracted to that person, knowing that he or she needs you as keenly as you need them.

Tell yourself that you are going to be alert to any Subconscious hunch which will give you the impulse to follow a certain lead, contact a certain firm or party, however fruitless your Conscious mind may try to convince you that your effort is.

What you call a "hunch" is often the method your Subconscious mind takes in putting you next to opportunities it has created for you in accordance with the mental blueprint you have given it to work out. Follow these hunches when you have learned how to detect the genuine ones, and let your Conscious mind determine the reason for them later.

Detach yourself from the situation entirely. Blank your conscious mind. Keep the "motion picture screen of your inner mind" open and clear. Relax your attitude physically and mentally and wait, quietly, for your Subconscious mind to flash its own picture or impression of what is going to happen or what is the best move for you to make. Any over-anxiety or wonderment or fear will awaken your imagination and cause it to produce the wrong picture ; and if you haven't learned how to distinguish between a picture or impression created by your imagination and one created by your Subconscious, you are apt to follow a wrong lead.

The best way to do—if you cannot consciously determine what course of action you should take or find it impossible to solve a problem—is to think it over carefully and then turn all the facts over to your Subconscious mind. Having done this, deliberately put the whole matter out of your Conscious mind and think about something else in the faith that your Subconscious mind will now go to work on your problem and create the right answer or solution for you.

You will be amazed, a little later, to receive a thought or idea which will come to you without any *conscious* thinking and which will point the way out. You can probably recall this already having happened to you many times. And you will find, whenever you have pursued a real hunch, that it has always led you correctly.

Repeat your visualizing of what you desire in life again and again. Your mental pictures will become stronger with each visualization and the thing visualized will be brought closer to you. And, one happy day, that day determined by the vividness and confidence behind your visualization, you will arrive at the moment when the objective pictured will have been achieved. But, long before that time, you will doubtless have picked out a new goal, preparing yourself for it and projecting new pictures beyond the now old ones. Then you will experience a new joy and thrill of living and come into the knowledge that a boundless, ever-widening opportunity is always before you, limited only by, your ability to grasp it through proper attunement of your Consciousness with the one great law of the Universe—the law of your Subconscious mind.

(b) Your Mind and Your Future

I know that many of you have great plans for your future. You feel that you are soon going to be able to capitalize upon your experiences of the past. You have probably looked over the things that have happened to you and, wherever you have made a mistake in judgment or desire, you have said to yourself: "I won't make *that* mistake again. I'm going to profit by the lesson that experience has taught me. I'm going to build my future on the mistakes of my past!"

If you have actually reached this stage of development wherein you are able to look at yourself as one looking in a mirror, with the courage to pick out your own weaknesses and defects and the will to go to work on them—no force on earth can keep you from greatly bettering your own condition.

I know many friends who make every effort to cover up their own faults. You would think that they were actually in love with their faults and, the truth really is, some of them are. But the same effort they expend trying to alibi and excuse their shortcomings would be sufficient to eliminate these failings if they only turned the effort in this direction. It is just as easy for you to form good habits as bad. But it is twice as difficult to break a habit once formed. That is because you have impressed this habit so strongly upon your inner or Subconscious mind that it automatically causes you to repeat it every time a similar situation arises in which the habit has played a part.

The only way you can break your habit is to picture yourself reacting normally and sensibly to whatever happens. See yourself, in your mind's eye, having overcome the bad habit, doing what you know you should do when the occasion demands. In this manner you will decrease the hold that the habit has upon you and, as you keep on visualizing yourself meeting each situation in the right way, you will finally have rid yourself of the bad habit entirely and replaced it with a good one.

In planning your future, it is necessary that you clear your mind of the debris, the destructive thoughts and impressions that you have stored there through the years. It will seem to you like cleaning out an old attic. As you look within yourself you will be amazed at the relics you will discover—outmoded ideas and wrong reactions to things that have been pushed into the attic of your mind, out of sight, many long since forgotten—but they have only served all this time to clutter up your clear thinking, to influence your present reactions to things and to keep you from going ahead as fast as you might.

A woman said to me not long ago, "I just don't ever seem to get around to the thing I want to do. My life is so filled with unnecessary activities—there are so many demands upon my time—and there is nothing I can do about it!"

Of course there isn't, so long as she pictures herself being helpless to change her condition. She is daily giving her Subconscious mind the thought that she can't get around to the thing she wants to do; and the Subconscious mind, her faithful servant, is seeing to it that she never does, since it can only bring to her what she orders.

The truth of the matter is, she really wants to do the things she is doing or she would see to it that she did something else! Naturally every human has certain responsibilities—certain tasks which would not be of the first choosing—but there is no reason why each one of us cannot begin to do the things we really want to do. It all depends upon our attitude of mind. If we can see ourselves, in our mind's eye, vividly and confidently, doing the thing that most appeals to us, it will not be long until circumstances and conditions are attracted to us, giving us the opportunity to develop the ability for that thing. Nothing can be denied you if you want it earnestly enough and are willing to put forth the effort to attain it. Your inner or Subconscious mind will supply the materials with which to build the future you visualize if you supply it with the right mental pictures to work from for you.

Abraham Lincoln wanted to become a lawyer badly enough to walk forty-four miles to borrow a volume of Blackstone's Commentaries. He walked nine miles every day to attend a crude log cabin school. No effort of body and mind was too great for him to spend in the attaining of an education. He saw himself securing a background of knowledge and experience which would fit him for big things in life; and his Subconscious mind, his obedient servant, molded his future for him.

Your future can only contain what you have built into your past-since you are laying the foundation now for that which is to happen tomorrow and the day after that and all days to come. It is your task to remove all weak stones from that foundation. Otherwise you may unconsciously be building a structure that will collapse and topple over upon you.

It is hard for anyone to realize the gathering force of each individual act as one experience is added to another. A series of wrong moves, each small in themselves, finally multiplies into a major catastrophe. It was the assassination of a little-known archduke that brought on World War I but conditions had been building toward such a happening for months and years; greed and hatred and national rivalries had reached the boiling point and this one act blew off the lid.

It is characteristic of our present system of living that we tax ourselves to the limit before we stop to read the handwriting on the wall. We abuse our bodies and fill our minds with mental pictures of fear and worry and then find it difficult to understand why we have suffered from a nervous breakdown.

You need not undergo any such experience if you take hold of yourself now. Clear your inner or Subconscious mind of all wrong mental pictures. See yourself starting out on a clean, fresh basis. You are not going to let your mistakes or failures of the past influence your future. Just because you have failed before is no reason for you to fail again unless you are afraid of failing and see a vivid picture of failure. Erase such pictures from the motion picture screen of your mind and visualize happy, successful pictures in their place.

Expect cheerful conditions around you. Look for agreeable companions. Show a sincere, wholehearted interest in the activities and problems of those dear to you-and they will respond by showing a helpful, understanding interest in your affairs. Your future is entirely what you make it. Once you have trained your mind it will think the kind of mental pictures that can bring you only good results. It will warn you instinctively every time a wrong mental picture or impression tries to gain entrance to your inner or Subconscious mind. You will be able to rule this wrong picture out by an effort of your will-thus preventing your Subconscious mind from working against you.

You will be surprised how quickly your present troubles will begin to disappear as you change your outlook. A well-to-do friend of mine who occupied a beautiful penthouse apartment which commanded a magnificent view of New York City's skyline, was suddenly deprived of his fortune and forced, almost overnight, to change his style of living drastically. He literally and figuratively came down to earth, moving from his top floor apartment to an apartment in the basement of the same building. Friends of his, who had formerly visited his penthouse for the purpose of enjoying the marvelous view which its terraces afforded, remarked to him, sympathetically, "Certainly tough, Fred. Bet you miss being up high and that gorgeous vista you had of New York!" But my friend smiled and shook his head. "Miss it?" he said. "Why should I miss it when I've a more wonderful view from where I am?

"I'm down here where I can study people; that old skyline never changed but here I see new and interesting sights every time I look out of my windows. Besides, living on the ground floor, I've gotten acquainted with many persons in the neighborhood; and I've discovered that the best view of all is what you see in others."

This friend had learned to adjust himself to external experience—had learned that happiness is not basically dependent upon certain surroundings or possessions. If he had clung, however, to a mental picture of his penthouse experience and compared it with his present living conditions, he would have had no eyes to see the advantages offered by his new situation. But, best of all, his wife saw things exactly as he did; she made the best of what might have been regarded as a calamity; and their home is one of the happiest drop-in places I know today.

A man and wife with this outlook cannot long remain confined, restricted or limited regarding physical things. If they can see beauty where others see nothing but drabness, all the beauty they desire will come to them; they can have it for the asking. In the case of this husband and wife, his affairs have now taken a turn for the better because he has constantly visualized himself making another fortune, yet they prefer to remain where they are when they could now afford some of their former luxuries.

Guard your own mental pictures. If you have suffered economic reversals or a severe personal upset, do not prolong your misery by continually reliving these experiences in your mind. Let go of the past and take hold of the future with its promise of everything in life you want or need. It is there for you the instant you can vividly and confidently picture it on that motion picture screen of your inner mind!

CHAPTER THREE

The Physical Side

A motorist, some time ago, boasted to me about the fine care he gave his automobile. He said that he had it completely overhauled regularly every six months, that he saw to it that the car had frequent changes of oil, the proper amount of air in the tires, and every detail attended to which would guarantee perfect performance.

"And would you believe it," this man said to me, "my car's ten years old? Yet it runs better than most of the new models my friends have bought!"

I looked at this man who boasted about his ten-year-old motor marvel and saw a physical wreck. His body congested by years of overeating and faulty elimination, he had failed to take much needed exercise; his muscles were flabby, his endurance so far below par that he puffed for breath when climbing a short flight of stairs. I could tell from his skin that his system was loaded with toxic poisons. Yet, there he was—under fifty years of age—and almost ready for the junk heap *physically*.

No wonder he was given to business worries and grumbled continually about poor conditions. He was low in body and spirit, and his one pride—his one and only pride—was the excellent care he gave his car.

In looking at this man I could not help but feel how utterly foolish so many of us are in giving abnormal attention to so many things in life that are not worth it. Perhaps he does not realize, even now, that unless he soon changes his way of living and thinking, he will not be in a position to enjoy either an old car or a new one.

Why is it that personal efficiency comes last in the planning of so many lives? Living in this mechanical age, we seem to think our bodies and minds will go on forever. That's why we see so many breakdowns at middle-age; that's why so many are prematurely old; burned out before life fairly begins. We race our human motors, develop "carbon" in our cylinders and valves, become "choked" with wrong thinking and wrong living, until Nature's remarkable handiwork, the human body, can no longer absorb the abuse. And all the while, simply obeying a few basic natural laws would have kept us in very good running order.

Your job, right at this moment, if you feel physically and mentally low, is to get busy on the quality and character of your mental pictures. A fear thought attacks your nerve centers, causing a chemical change—the creation of toxic poisons—which react destructively upon your whole system. On the contrary, a courageous or optimistic thought invigorates; it stimulates these same nerve centers and brings about a healthy chemicalizing of your body.

There is no question but that your health and your youth are definitely influenced by your mind. And because of this it is well to know that: age is not a matter of years, it is a matter of outlook; health is not a matter of physique, it is a matter of physical and mental disciplining.

Some of the happiest and most long-lived people are those who have suffered a chronic affliction for years. Their very affliction has imposed upon them the necessity of eating, drinking, working, playing and sleeping in moderation and this, in turn, has rewarded them with better health than those who are apparently free from bodily ills.

If you are bemoaning a poor state of health, you may not yet have learned how to capitalize upon that which you now regard as a misfortune and a severe handicap.

Everything happens for the best in the great ultimate of things. We must believe this if we are to believe that we are dwellers in a rational Universe. The trouble too often is that we are too close to our problems and misfortunes to extract the constructive lesson or value and permit, instead, our perspective to become distorted. It may require years before, looking back with our mind mellowed and our emotions softened, we are able to say: "I wouldn't change the pattern now if I could. The things that have befallen me, I now see that I have brought upon myself. But for certain hardships I would never have developed certain strengths. But for certain sorrows, I would not have known certain moments of gladness. Life itself is well ordered—it is, when all is said and done, exactly what I have made it. I have only myself to blame or praise."

But, you may be one who has been sickly from birth. You may have been born an invalid; born deaf, dumb or blind or paralyzed. And you are saying, "What has there been in my life for me? How can I say that life has been fair, that I have been given an equal chance with others, that I am responsible for my condition?"

There is only one feasible, understandable answer to this very logical question.

If this one life were *all*, then you would have every right to damn creation, to denounce what appears to you as the imperfection and cruelty of Nature. But I am positive this physical existence is only the beginning of a continuing life experience which reaches beyond the state we call "death."

In this next dimension, the physical inequalities of this life are evened up and you will find yourself to possess a perfected body form, no longer deformed or subject to pain.

God, the Great Intelligence, did not decree that you should be born with, or develop physical deformities or ills here. In His wisdom, He permitted you to be born in accordance with the physical laws of cause and effect established on this planet. If you had been created perfect, with no freedom of choice, no will to decide between the right and wrong way of thinking and acting, you would have been forever deprived of the glorious power to develop and possess your own soul through life experience. You would operate on a mechanical level only.

So, if certain physical causes have given you a damaged fleshly house in which to live, do not bemoan your fate but make the best of it, secure in the faith that life holds more for you than you dream even here on earth—if you will maintain the right mental attitude. And, as for the future, exercise this same faith to believe and know that your entity or real self will occupy another body of finer substance, in the life to come, a life which will be as real to you then as this one is now.

It is the way you react to your experiences here, no matter what your physical handicaps may be, which counts! Your soul is being evolved by the decisions you make, what you think and do. Your personality, your identity, the "I am I" of you remains the same. But your capacity for the development of truth and understanding and all of the qualities which your consciousness needs to prepare you for the life beyond is growing with each new worthwhile experience.

It is up to you to see to it that you make proper choice of the experiences you have in life. If you choose wisely, the experiences you bring to you can contribute much to your own advancement in wisdom and character.

The duties and responsibilities of this life are of first importance but it is our right attention to these matters which determines largely our soul's evolution. Live a starved, self-centered life and your soul will reflect these attributes, for your soul is the real you! Such faults as you still possess will have to be worked out in the training school of your next life. Compensation must be made for every misstep. You can attract to yourself nothing that has not been attained within.

So, resolve to take full advantage of the opportunities offered you in this earthly kindergarten in order that you may be ready to partake of the greater joys possible to you when you graduate, through death, to the next conscious phase of your soul's progressive existence.

Think long and deeply upon the above explanation. If medical science is powerless to help you, then give yourself over to your Mind. Retire to the inner sanctum of the greatest power that is or ever can be. Get acquainted with this Inner Self. Clear up the distortions in consciousness which are reflected in the distortions of your physical body. And, while you in this lifetime, may or may not be able to generate sufficient visualizing power to overcome your physical disability, you can most certainly have corrected your inner concept and erased many warped impressions which have come as a result of a wrong reaction to a misshapen exterior.

So-called miracles have been achieved by correction of a mental attitude. It is necessary for each of us, in order to make the hardships and sufferings of life bearable, to discover the constructive reason behind things. If the world in which we live appears to have no rhyme or reason, then the experiences we are called upon to undergo mean nothing to us but misery.

"If I could only faintly discern the working out of a Divine or Infinite plan in the life of Man, I would accept all that comes to me with patience and with fortitude," said a friend. "For I would know that it all has a place in the great scheme of things and that each experience, however bitter or sweet, was meant, by a great divine plan, to leave its impress upon my soul."

When health abounds, when youth surges in one's physical body, life takes on a rosy hue. God is in His heaven and all is well with the world. We do not require much of a philosophy then to meet the ordinary issues of the day. Health gives to us the temporary glow of immortality. We have to give pause and think back to realize that there was a time when we apparently "were not"—a time prior to our earthly birth when no man could have predicted that we would exist. We give as little heed to the march of time in the other direction—some moment in the future when this body will be laid aside, either a worn-out garment or one that has outserved its usefulness.

Life is a school from which humans are constantly graduating in Consciousness. Life is a turbulent stream which we must learn to breast, and which—once we have developed within us the power to ride the waves—bears us majestically along to higher and finer things!

(*a*) Nothing Happens by Accident

Do you realize how much it would mean to you if you could be sure that nothing ever happens by accident? That you are living in a world so well ordered that not the slightest thing happens without there being an exact cause behind it? That you, yourself, are the maker of your own destiny, consciously or unconsciously attracting the circumstances which surround you, either for your own good or bad!

I know it is going to be hard for you, at first, to accept this as actually the case. I know you are going to feel, as you look back over your life and try to determine why certain things had to happen, that you couldn't have been responsible for many of them; that life, for some reason beyond your control, had seen fit to abuse you or visit upon you certain experiences that you would never have chosen. And yet, in unguarded moments, your fears and worries have pictured these conditions so intensely that your Inner Mind, with its power to create what you picture, has been compelled to bring these conditions upon you.

Perhaps the exact happening has not been pictured by you but a general fear of a condition has made you susceptible to any one of a number of happenings growing out of this condition. Remember always, that your Subconscious mind is a faithful servant possessing the power to produce for you whatever you vividly visualize. Keeping this in mind, you will be able to understand why so many business men die shortly after announcing their retirement from business. They have mentally pictured, for years, arriving at the end of their life's work. They have seen, in their mind's eye, the day when they could say, "It is finished." And, very foolishly, they have *not* pictured themselves partaking in any activity beyond their business life. As a consequence, the Subconscious mind accepts the fact that their life work is done and sets about its task of completing the picture—letting go its hold upon life.

Some years ago, while a resident of Marion, Indiana, I knew an educator by the name of Professor Clayton. He had long been associated with the public school system and was beloved by fellow teachers and students throughout the state. As he was the senior professor in standpoint of years, he was made chairman of the state convention of high school teachers which was held in Marion.

At this convention, Professor Clayton was to make the feature address. He was naturally pleased and thrilled at the honor and had chosen, as his concluding remarks, a poem from the historic McGuffey's Fifth Reader. This poem touchingly recalled the years of service, applying in a personal way to all teachers present.

Professor Clayton felt greatly moved as he recited. Those who heard him said that his voice quavered and tears came to his eyes as he entered upon the passage which referred to dear friends of former days, and which read:

We are not all here
There are those who are gone,
But we go on and on . . .

And, with his repeating of these lines, Professor Clayton suddenly sagged forward and fell to the floor, *dead!*

While in a highly emotional state, he had visualized the possibility of his own demise—and his Subconscious mind, reacting instantly to his strong mental picture, had brought about a nerve reaction which had reached his heart.

And if you think this was a mere coincidence, let me tell you of another case-exactly similar, which occurred a short time ago in Whitehouse, New Jersey. *The New York Times*, in reporting the sudden death of William Doyle Ditmars, a member of the lower house of the Ohio legislature, told of his being present at a family reunion. Addressing members of the Ditmars-Stryker Association, of which he was president, Mr. Ditmars stood near a table on the lawn. "He collapsed," the *Times* went on to say, "just after reciting these words of a poem in McGuffey's Fifth Reader:

We are not all here,
There are those who are gone,
But we go on and on . . .

It is apparent, from these strikingly parallel cases, that the Subconscious mind reacts mathematically the same in every consciousness when influenced by the same kind of impression. Thus, the words of the poem had caused Mr. Ditmars to picture, as Professor Clayton had done some years before, his own demise. And conditions were emotionally and physically just right for the mental picture to be executed at once!

There is no such thing as coincidence in a universe that operates in accordance with certain mental and physical laws. There are many happenings which we find difficult to explain by a surface examination but you may rest assured there is a basic cause behind them and they are not the happenstances they appear.

"If So and So had done thus and so, it wouldn't have happened," has often been remarked. But the fact remains that So and So did not do thus and so—and that which happened was inevitably the result!

Look for the cause back of everything that occurs to you. Check back over your past and see if you can discover a mental attitude which unconsciously attracted certain conditions to you. Examine your Inner Mind and determine the nature of your present thought pictures which are stored there. You will find some that you will recognize immediately as wrong in character—capable of influencing the creative power within you to bring a wrong condition to pass in your life.

Get busy the instant a wrong mental picture is discovered, erase it from your consciousness and replace it with the right kind of mental picture, wherein you see yourself freed of such a situation or overcoming the fear of it. If you do not, and if you permit yourself to visualize similar mental pictures, you may expect, one of these days, to see these things happen to you in your actual life.

A happy, optimistic state of mind in the face of obstacles generates a force within that can combat these obstacles and enable you once more to see clearly, to act intelligently and get the results desired in place of continuing the victim of your own depressed thoughts and the conditions they, have attracted.

If your tendency has been to blame others and forces without yourself for what has befallen you—or if you've laid it all to "hard luck"—put these negative mental attitudes aside and take hold of yourself, determined to change the entire outlook within a short span of time. It *can* be done. And you will take heart in the realization that there is no such thing as an accident, that there is a motivating force behind even the most trivial happening.

You will take heart because your reason will tell you that, if nothing is basically an accident, you actually can control your own destiny and, to a large degree, everything that the future holds in store for you—dependent only upon your ability to reach and direct, with vivid pictures, your inner or Subconscious mind!

(b) The Part that Faith Plays

I have been asked many times how great a part the exercise of faith plays in the achieving of that which you desire. This inquiry was particularly prompted by newspaper reports of the mountain preacher who held a rattlesnake aloft in his pulpit and permitted it to strike him. The snake twice buried its fangs in his upraised arm but the preacher, suffering intense pain, refused medical treatment, declaring that his faith would take care of it.

The arm burst from swelling; his tongue was so swollen that it almost choked him; he lay near death while his mountain congregation prayed for his recovery. It was the belief of these simple folk that their pastor would not even have been bitten by the rattlesnake except that he must have had a "little doubt" in his mind, had momentarily lost a little of his faith or else had done something wrong. But the minister, fanatically maintaining his belief in the power of faith, fought off the ravages of the rattlesnake venom in his system, and arose from his bed to preach to his clan the following Sunday, proclaiming himself as a "living example of what faith can do."

With the knowledge you now possess of how your Inner Mind actually operates, you perhaps are able to analyze for yourself the part that this pastor's mind really played in his recovery.

In the first place it is helpful to know that, according to Raymond L. Ditmars, curator of reptiles at the Bronx Zoo, only fifteen percent of persons bitten by rattlesnakes actually die. This means that, spectacular as the case may have sounded, the minister—providing he possessed excellent health and a good physique—had an eighty-five percent chance to survive.

Despite this, Mr. Ditmars, speaking of this case, said, "I believe that the Reverend's mental state, bolstered by his religious belief and faith, aided him considerably."

There is no question but that *faith* is one of the strongest forces we can command—faith in the creative power within us. But this faith should not be tested foolishly or needlessly. The wife of this same minister died several years ago in childbirth, spurning the aid of a medical doctor. Her faith did not save her since she refused to make use of scientific methods developed by the mind of man from this same God-given inner creative source; scientific methods which were designed to serve and liberate humanity.

It becomes very evident, then, that there are two kinds of faith—*blind* faith and faith based upon *true* knowledge. Even blind faith has a strong reactionary effect upon your physical body; but it is not based upon fact and where a situation is dependent upon certain factors beyond ordinary physical control, blind faith is seldom sufficient to overcome a condition.

You are, of course, familiar with the saying, "Faith, without works, is dead."

And this is what blind faith really is: "faith without works." True faith is not guesswork, it is not a dependence upon so-called happenstance, nor is it the idle belief that you can sit down and picture things coming to you without making any effort to bring them. You must back up your faith that you are capable of achieving a certain end by *working* toward that end with every energy and faculty at your command!

This minister had a supreme faith that enabled him to survive the poisonous venom of the rattlesnake. He saw an intense mental picture of his being able to fight off the effects of the poison without the aid of any combative serum or medical attention. The members of his congregation, feeling a strong bond of sympathy for him, *prayed*—visualizing vivid mental pictures of their pastor's recovery. This mental attitude maintained by the preacher and his congregation definitely contributed toward the overcoming of the minister's serious condition. All week long he kept repeating: "I'll be in my pulpit next Sunday as usual!" And this mental picture impressed upon his Inner Mind gave it added impetus in helping bring about a recovery which would permit the pastor to occupy his pulpit as he had visualized.

Strong fear thoughts as to the possibility of his recovery would, however, have complicated his condition and might even have so unnerved and devitalized him as to have cost him his life.

Very recently a Westerner, caught out on the prairie after dark, stumbled and was pricked on the leg by a cactus plant. Knowing himself to be in a region infested with rattlesnakes, he concluded that he had been bitten. Found some hours later in a weak and terrorized condition, the Westerner's body gave every external evidence of reaction to poison. When it was proven to him that he had not been bitten, the snakebite symptoms disappeared within an hour and the man recovered. But this aptly demonstrates the amazing influence of the mind upon the physical body.

The power this mountain preacher called upon to "save" him was this creative power within himself; the same creative power that exists within us all. It is a universal force, a force upon which man has drawn from the day of his creation up to the present moment, a force capable of unlimited accomplishments if it is not abused or misdirected.

This creative power is *in* and *behind* everything in this Universe. It is the power that unites the elements and produces worlds. Some call it the God force; others call it Infinite Intelligence; still others refer to it as Universal Consciousness.

It matters not what name you call it, but it is there and you are a part of it. This creative power is not ruled by Time or Space. It will continue to exist after your physical body has been laid to rest. And your *Real Self,* a part of this creative power, will also continue to exist.

Nothing can basically die. This is a universe of change, of development, of progress. You and I have always existed as a part of this universe or we couldn't be here today. We were included in the creative scheme of things, however small and unimportant we may seem.

Radio engineers will tell you that radio waves will continue to vibrate in space, even though they cannot be reached and recaptured by your receiving set. Nothing is fundamentally lost. Everything has its place in the universe. Each of us is just as closely associated with this creative power ; the more we know of it, the more we strive to understand our Inner Self, the more ready we will be to meet the problems of this life and to face the great adventure of the change called *Death!*

This creative power within us, however, is *not* a toy to be played with. It should not be flaunted, put on display or jokingly called upon. For this creative power has no sense of humor. It takes whatever you mentally picture seriously and starts to materialize it for you.

It pays you back in the same coin you give it. And, while individuals like this minister can occasionally demonstrate successfully the influence of mind upon the body, one who truly understands and respects the operation of this inner creative power does not purposely endanger his or her life for the purpose of trying to demonstrate to others how the power works.

Each day there are thousands of unrecorded instances where humans everywhere are exercising faith in the meeting of difficult situations—*seeing* themselves overcoming conditions, *believing* earnestly in their ability to rise above certain obstacles—and this *faith,* this inner *knowing* that they possess the power to achieve their goal, has influenced their Subconscious minds to attract the necessary resources to them; resources which, coupled with their own wholehearted efforts, have enabled them to make their mental pictures come true. . As you study the lives and experiences of those about you, remembering how mathematically accurate is the operation of human mind, you will be able to understand why certain things have happened to your friends. You will be capable of analyzing a situation and determining what was the mental attitude of an individual which attracted this situation to him.

Unfortunately, due to the average lack of emotional control, it is much easier to have faith that something bad is going to happen than it is to have faith that everything is going to work out happily and successfully. This is because our minds have been so filled with pictures of distress and past failures that we unconsciously couple these with the bright pictures we are trying to paint of our future.

Faith is a deep-seated feeling that a certain thing is going to happen, however impossible its happening may appear at the moment. Faith, for that reason, is closely associated with your emotions and, to control the nature of your faith, it is necessary that you control your emotions by eliminating fear and worry thoughts.

Faith is the priceless ability to believe in yourself; to be consciously aware that you possess God-given creative power within yourself and sufficient knowledge of how to call upon it to overcome all external conditions. With such a faith and the intelligent application of it, your fears and worries must vanish and the good things in life *must* come!

CHAPTER FOUR

Fear: How to Control It

*F*ear results from your feeling of inability to face a definite situation. You see a mental picture of yourself in a dangerous position, up against it financially, deathly sick or embarrassed at the thought of meeting certain people and, sure enough, the things you have been afraid would happen eventually come to pass!

I have told you that you possess a creative power which has no reasoning faculty and which brings to you whatever you mentally picture. If you vividly and confidentially picture good things happening, this creative power sees to it that good things do happen; if you picture bad things occurring, the creative power takes for granted that you want bad things to take place, and so sets about to attract these conditions to you.

Like, as I have repeatedly said, attracts like. You get back in life, ultimately, exactly what you give out. This is all controlled by the one great mental law. There is no more striking evidence of its operation than in the kidnapping of the married daughter of one of Kentucky's most prominent and wealthy families.

Behind this kidnapping was a family fear existing since her birth, that this very thing would happen. As a baby, elaborate precautions for her protection were taken by the parents who, as *The New York Times* reported, "realized that their fortune might be a magnet to draw ill to them."

The garden where the baby had her airings was surrounded by a high spiked fence. She was watched by an unfailing nurse. When the little girl started to school she went to a private institution across the alley from her own home. Even so, she was always escorted to and from the schoolhouse by the family chauffeur.

Outside of school hours, she was not allowed to run down to the corner for a soda. She never went with other girls to movies or wandered with them through the beautiful park nearby. She was accompanied to her friends' homes in the afternoon by a maid.

After her wedding, the young woman continued the vigilance on which she was brought up. Her husband built a home on the outskirts of the town, where safeguards against invaders were taken. She practiced shooting a pistol. Three large beacon lights were installed to light the grounds at night and a large and fierce dog was bought.

In addition to these protective measures, three servants were on duty on the estate. But, on the day a man kidnapped her, the butler was in town, the yardman far away across the grounds, and the maid was tied up by the invader. The dog was ill.

Life is filled with such examples if we will but look for them—and we do not have to look beyond ourselves because we are reaping the harvest of past fears and worries every day of our lives.

Just now we may only be paying a physical penalty. Our fears may be upsetting our nerves, affecting our digestion, keeping us from sleeping nights, or nagging us so that we really can't enjoy anything we may be doing.

But now that you can see and understand how your mind really operates you are certainly not going to continue worrying about the possibility of something happening to you, knowing that this mental attitude greatly strengthens the chances of its happening!

It required years for the fears of this wealthy family and their daughter to be realized, but they ultimately came to pass! Her husband, the intended victim, was not at home, which left the kidnaper with the alternative of taking the wife. Thus, she finally found herself in the situation she had mentally pictured, all conditions had at last been made perfect despite the best laid plans to prevent it. This experience should prove, beyond a doubt, the infallible operation of the law of attraction. No material force can stand against it, once this law is put in motion.

Your greatest protection is your attitude of mind. If you are picturing dire things happening to husband or wife or loved ones—stop this mental visualizing at once! Picture, instead, no one having any desire to think ill of them or taking any action against them. Remember: things first happen in the mind of man before they can happen in this external world. The basic cause of conditions you are constantly encountering exists in the mind. If your loved ones are free of personal fears and if they have done nothing to invite the malice of others there is no way that certain harmful acts can be attracted to them.

No human was ever born who did not know the sensation of fear. In the young, fear sometimes serves a useful purpose, since it develops a sense of caution. The mature or adult mind, however, was not meant to be dominated by undirected emotions, nor was it intended to be ruled by fear. And yet the majority of us are slaves to one fear or another.

Most of your fears are carryovers from childhood. You have simply failed to overcome or outgrow the early impressions which were made upon you by a startling experience.

You fear that which you have not conquered in yourself. Some of us are strong where others are weak and weak where others are strong. Certain fears that you have defeated may still plague the next person. Something that would not concern them in the slightest, might bring terror to you.

Fear indicates a lack of balance between your outer and inner self. Your fears, implanted in consciousness, remain hidden away until a new similar happening revives or resurrects them. And each time you are reminded of an unconquered fear, the effect of this fear upon you only adds to its destructive force.

Here is an interesting check you can make to determine how many everyday fears dominate you! Answer "yes" or "no" if you are obsessed with

> Fear of being up high
> Fear of falling
> Fear of water
> Fear of certain animals
> Fear of thunder and lightning
> Fear of fire
> Fear of the dark
> Fear of crowds
> Fear of disease
> Fear of meeting people
> Fear of what others may think
> Fear of being alone
> Fear of poverty
> Fear of "the worst always happening"
> Fear of being locked in a room
> Fear of what may befall loved ones
> Fear of pain and death

This does not begin to list the fears to which the average human is heir. But, if any of these fears have a hold upon you, it is because your uncontrolled emotions cause you mentally to picture yourself in a situation which you feel you cannot meet.

Your emotions, gripping your consciousness, destroy your Will to act, and make you an easy prey to the thing feared. You feel you are powerless to master this fear because you have not mastered it successfully in the past.

Life's experiences are intended to make you eventually face yourself—face *reality*. But it is human nature for you to want to put off unpleasant admissions of weaknesses in yourself as long as possible. The longer, however, that you postpone checking up on yourself, the greater penalty you will pay for humoring your faults and the harder it will be to break yourself of them.

Your first step in the removal of fear from your consciousness is your ability to analyze yourself, to look back upon incidents on your life when you were gripped by fear—reliving these incidents in your mind's eye. This will enable you to see clearly what your proper emotional reaction should have been. You will notice that the same sensation of fear you experienced at the time will be sensed by you as you recall each happening. This will prove to you that the fear is still alive within you, ready to break out with intensified force the next time another situation arises like the ones you have faced.

To do away with this fear, you should, while mentally reliving these moments, *see* yourself having conquered your emotions. Replace the mental pictures your mind has stored away on past failures to control your fear by mental pictures of this fear being dominated by you.

Practice daily, repeating courageous thought pictures of yourself facing situations which have downed you in your past, as you know you *should* have faced them. In time you will have built such a strong thought structure that your fears will be entirely walled out.

Aviators, perhaps without knowing the law of the Subconscious mind, nevertheless realize that they must overcome a wrong mental picture or it will develop in them a fear complex that may result disastrously.

Whenever a student pilot has cracked up in a plane, if he has not been injured, he is commanded by his superior officer to get in another ship immediately and take to the air again that he may *erase* the memory of his crash landing.

If you have been troubled with a fear of being up high, the next time you are in a tall building or upon a lofty elevation, try this. Consciously visualize the firm, safe position of your body in place of permitting your mind to picture the possibility of your body falling through space. Only one mental picture can be held in your consciousness at any one moment and this picturing of yourself' as absolutely safe will crowd out your customary fear picture. If you look straight down from this height, do not mentally take your body to the street with your vision. Let your eye alone cover the distance from where you are to the street, while *you* remain consciously aware that your body is safely rooted in your present position. A little practice of this mental attitude will free you from fear of heights and falling.

When you have convinced yourself inwardly that many of your fears are childish and groundless, that they only weaken you and make every situation you face the more unbearable, you will have dealt your fears a mental blow from which they cannot recover. It is you who must kill them off if you would not have them, in time, destroy you. Fear attracts wrong conditions; courage repels these same conditions and attracts the right ones in their place.

You who suffer from a fear of electrical storms, let me show you how Reason can destroy such a fear. Do you realize that your own mind is actually an *electrical machine?* You have heard of the marvelous experiments wherein the electrical activity of gray matter, the thinking apparatus of the brain and seat of intelligence, was demonstrated. Did you know that there is a constant electrical activity going on in the living brain, and that rhythmic electrical changes are occurring, night and day, even in the *absence* of any external happening?

Do you, who fear electrical storms, realize what this

means? You are fearing the manifestation of something which exists within your own consciousness! The entire world is made up of electrical vibrations which have taken different external forms. And when we humans permit fear and hate and greed and anger and other destructive emotions to grip us, we are creating *electrical storms* within *ourselves!* We are over-charging our brains with emotional vibrations. Our battery of brain cells is unable to handle these electrical vibrations at the moment so that a short-circuit is caused. We find our Conscious mind paralyzed. We are unable to think or act—we have been cut off from this electrical power within-we cannot receive the ordinary impulses in the form of ideas from our inner mind or the great Subconscious *powerhouse.*

You can *demagnetize,* by the right mental attitude, any conditions that you formerly have attracted to yourself through wrongly created electrical vibrations in your own consciousness. When you have so much power within you, why not commence using it for *constructive* rather than destructive purposes?

Fear need not rule you. Take command of yourself and, by applying this mental method to your own specific fears, drive them from your consciousness and your life forever.

(*a*) Worry: a Handmaiden of Fear

It is human nature to worry. Almost as natural for most persons to worry as to breathe. But it is high time, just the same, if you are the worrying kind, that you should be doing something about it.

Worry, and its ally, Fear, mars more happiness and brings about more grief than all other wrong emotions combined.

An emotion is only wrong when it is used wrongly; and you are certainly misusing your emotions when you play upon them with your constant worries as to what may happen. Worry destroys self-confidence, dampens your enthusiasm, causes you to be hesitant and undecided about things, takes the edge off your simple enjoyment of everyday affairs and often upsets you physically. And yet, knowing all this, you go right on worrying! Why do you do it?

I have asked many people just that question and they have replied: "How can I help it?" And to such people my answer has been: "You can help it only by getting better acquainted with yourself so that you can understand the reason for your worrying. You admit to me that most of your worries are needless—that few of the things you worry about actually happen—and yet you continue to worry!"

And the reason you continue to worry is that you haven't learned to control your emotions. Things have happened to you in the past that have frightened you or disturbed you and these happenings have left their impressions in your mind. Now, without realizing it, every time something occurs to remind you of this happening, you commence worrying for fear it may happen again. Your present attitude toward the things you have to face in life is determined by your past reaction to similar happenings. You must always remember that you think in terms of mental pictures. You have been storing mental pictures away in your Subconscious mind for many years.

This Subconscious mind of yours is like a filing cabinet. It contains a record of your every thought and act. And it is constantly adding to this record. It is receiving the thoughts you are getting from these pages. It is the part of you that never sleeps. It controls the functioning of your body-the beating of your heart, your breathing, your digestion-and does its job perfectly so long as you do not interfere with it by thinking worry or fear thoughts.

You have often heard friends say, "I've worried myself sick!" They had crowded their conscious mind with so many pictures of failure or possible adversity that these depressing pictures had reached the Subconscious mind which, in turn, communicated them to the nervous system and an upset stomach was the result, or even a heart attack.

You can easily recall certain occasions when a sudden happening has so startled you that your heart has commenced pounding. This proves how closely related your inner or Subconscious mind is to the various vital organs of your body and how important it is not to permit your Subconscious mind to receive intense fear and worry thoughts. If you do, you will notice an almost immediate effect upon your health, and continued fear and worry is very apt to bring about a nervous breakdown.

Mothers are the world's worst worriers and, this, too, is only human since their worrying habit starts over their children. It is natural for a mother to be concerned over her youngsters and exceedingly difficult, because of a mother's emotional attachment for the child, for her to keep her feelings within bounds. But mothers should realize that worry never helps and often hinders. There have been many cases where worry has actually led to the thing feared really happening. This has been brought about by a mother's fears being passed on to her child and developing a timidity which has made the child more susceptible to possible mishaps or misadventures.

Most of us are worrying about the future so much that we can't enjoy our present—not stopping to realize that our present is all there is. The future never comes. When what we have thought of as a future time arrives, it is our present. And, if we haven't learned to be free of worry and fear, if we haven't changed our mental attitude and begun confidently and vividly to picture good things coming to us, then our future is going to be just as cheerless and filled with trouble as our past may have been.

The right mental attitude is going to lift a burden from your body and mind. You are going to enjoy life as you never have before, relieved of the tension and strain of worry. *Know* that this creative power within you, rightly directed, can protect you from many things you now fear. Give it the opportunity to go to work for you by picturing good things happening. Do not permit yourself to get emotionally upset as you formerly have. Take things calmly.

If you are not able to conquer your feelings entirely at first, every time you repeat the right mental attitude you will find yourself stronger and more capable of meeting the same situation next time. And, in time, you will have thrown off your fears and worries for good! When this time arrives, you will then know the meaning of true happiness!

(*b*) Neurotic Tendencies

Many individuals, under the stress and strain of modern-day living, are plagued by neurotic tendencies or actual neurotic conditions. A woman in Rhode Island wrote me some months ago, saying, "I am physically perfect but always just two jumps ahead of a nervous breakdown, which I can ill afford as I have my living to earn as a nurse. What can I do to be happy and normal mentally and rid myself of two phobias— fear of going insane and fear of going on the street alone? I laugh at these fears when I am all right and declare I will never slip again; but I am the exact duplicate of my neurotic father, who thought that I, being his daughter, must have all his weaknesses. Is it true that I must be neurotic because my father was?"

My answer to her may prove an answer to a similar mental state which is troubling yourself or a loved one. I said, "No, it doesn't follow that because you are a daughter of a neurotic father you yourself have to be neurotic. As a girl you have been so impressed by your father's weaknesses and later by your studies as a nurse, that you have come to believe yourself a victim of hereditary tendencies. But instead of this, you are actually the victim of mental suggestion.

"You've been mentally picturing the possibility of yourself going insane or being unable to face the pressure of certain circumstances. This has developed in you a fear which becomes strongest when you are over-tired, since your nerves are then on edge and your mind is much more sensitive to disturbances around you. When things are going all right, you have a feeling of security which controls these phobias within you. But you need to face the exact cause of your condition and to eliminate it once and for all.

"The way to do this is to realize that your Subconscious or inner mind is only what you make it by your conscious thoughts. In other words, if you continually impress on your Subconscious mind that you are about to go insane and that you are afraid to go on the street alone, you are virtually ordering this inner creative power to produce these conditions for you.

"Your fear of going on the street alone is definitely related to your fear of losing your mind, since both fears concern your encountering an unknown and unexpected happening over which you feel you would have no control. You should understand that your inner self is mentally balanced and can only become unbalanced by your forcing upon it the fears, worries and apprehensions of your Conscious mind.

Knowing, then, that there is nothing wrong, as you say, physically, and that your inner consciousness or real self is perfectly normal, you have now only to control your outer mental attitude or Conscious mind in relation to this inner self in order to eliminate your phobias that have actually no existence in fact—and must lose their hold upon you the instant you have recognized that they are only products of your imagination."

Insanity, resulting from mental causes, is brought about when *conscious* or *directional* control over one's Subconscious or inner mind is lost. It cannot happen unless you, yourself, permit it. And those who suffer from a fear of being on the street alone should realize that they are not actually alone. They are in the company of this creative power *within,* which is ready to protect and care for them at all times, once they have learned to rely upon it.

More humans than is generally realized are suffering from an upset mental condition of one kind or another. Another woman wrote me the following: "I am now sixty-five years of age and have spent five years in a State Hospital for the Insane.

When I became mentally ill or suffered a *nervous breakdown* as it is kindly called, my family could not afford to send me to a private hospital. I realized my condition and wanted help.

"The State Hospital was the only place to go. I committed myself, much to my regret, after I had been there a few days. No treatment seemed given, and I realized, if I ever was to go home it was up to *me*. I was in for *melancholia*—and I had a hard time to get my mind on pleasant things.

"I only want to add—I've been home ten years and am treated as if I were normal, as I believe I am, and am happier than I have ever been in my life.

"I hope you will impress those who may be in need of mental help that it is *not* easy; and I pray that your wonderful suggestions may prevent others from undergoing an experience similar to mine."

You will note that this woman wishes it emphasized that recovering one's emotional and mental balance is "not easy." Of course it isn't easy—not when you may have been unconsciously operating your mind wrongly for years. But think of the joy you will experience in knowing that there is a way out of your troubles! Who wouldn't gladly put forth every effort once it is shown that the effort is immensely worthwhile? Few of you, reading these lines, will be called upon to make the mental effort required by her, and if you should chance to be on the verge of a nervous breakdown, you can check yourself in time.

If your nerves are on edge, if life has seemed almost too much for you, listen to me. I'm going to talk to you now as though your inner self, the creative power within you, were talking, and saying:

"Be still—be quiet—let your nerves be calmed—relaxed— for I, your Inner Self, am going to take control. You've tried to do without me all these years, you've scarcely known I existed, but now that things have gone wrong in your outer world, now that you've lost faith in worldly things, you think you don't know where to turn. You've at last come to the time in your life when you can face your *real* self, and you're going to discover that conditions aren't nearly as bad as you've pictured them. You possess a creative power within which will change all your outer conditions and surroundings and restore your confidence, your faith in life, and living.

"Don't argue. Don't try to reason or wonder. Just *accept* me—this force you feel within yourself. Let me go to work for you. I'm ready and willing. I've been ready and willing ever since you were born—more and more every year of your life. And all you have to do is to give me the right kind of mental pictures to go to work on.

"I can't change your life, bring you the things you desire, unless you picture them. As long as your mind has been filled with fear and worry, you've forced me to work against you—to bring what you've feared to pass in your life. But you didn't realize this; you thought all the time that some outside force was doing this to you; and that was because you didn't really understand yourself. You and I, your Inner Self, weren't really acquainted with one another. Now everything is going to be different. We know each other for the first time, and what a joy it is; how happy we're going to be, knowing that we can start now working together, making up for lost time, doing and having the things that should have been ours long, long ago!

There can't be any more despondency, despair and hopeless feelings. Life can't be empty any more; because you have *me,* your Inner Self, to rely upon, to lean upon, to call upon. And I have the power to bring you light, even in your darkest moments, if you will do away with your fear and worry thoughts and come to me at once, giving me the mental picture of what you need to overcome your difficulty.

"A great spiritual leader once said: 'Lo, I am with you always!' He was referring to this same great, God-given creative force within, and you now know how to use it. Spend some time with me, your Inner Self, each day. Talk your problems over with me; take counsel with your Inner Self; let me send hunches or flash ideas into your Conscious mind as to what you should do. I won't fail you, if you don't fail me. I'll reveal a new world to you in place of your present world of trouble. *Try* me! Try me *wholeheartedly!* Place your confidence in me and see how quickly conditions commence to improve about you!"

This is the way your Inner Self, your inner voice, will talk to you when you have made your mind receptive; when you have deliberately put aside the wear and tear of this life and gotten off for a few moments by yourself. The answer to your perplexing problems is within you, not without. You were born with a creative power sufficient to meet every situation in life as it should be met—sufficient to bring you happiness, health and all good things—once you have learned *how* to direct this God-given force within.

Remember, the path to greater happiness than you have ever experienced is not easy since you are the one who must take the steps on this path! But you are no longer stumbling in the dark, you now know the way. You know that you think in terms of mental pictures, that you have been getting out of life just what you have been visualizing, and that a changed mental attitude means a changing of your entire life.

Dare to feel that good things are coming to you. Dare to believe that you can lift yourself above present seeming obstacles. Dare to place your faith in this creative power within you. Dare to keep this faith alive through whatever you are undergoing. Dare to be cheerful with things apparently going against you. Soon, as you see the results you will begin to attain, it won't be necessary to take on this attitude. It will have become *second nature* with you to meet life courageously and confidently . . . *minus* the fears and worries that may now beset you!

CHAPTER FIVE

Taking Life Too Seriously

*D*o you take life too seriously? Do you let little things of no real consequence disturb you? Do you lie awake nights worrying about your conditions and picturing even worse things happening? And, even when you are able to have a good time or take things more easily, are you constantly telling yourself that you can't afford it, that you shouldn't be doing what you are, and that you will probably suffer tomorrow for what you have dared enjoy today?

I know many, many people who are like that. People who are unconsciously spoiling their lives and the lives of those around them because they are taking life too seriously. No one has ever yet aided a situation by worrying about it; nor has anyone ever improved their health by worrying over their physical condition. But, despite the fact that most people realize the harm and unhappiness they are bringing upon themselves by their worries and fears, very few of them make an earnest effort to take a new mental attitude toward life.

We all need a sense of humor in these times to give us the proper balance. The ability to relax and make light of a situation which has magnified itself in our itself in our minds is a great aid toward overcoming it. Something usually happens the instant we really "let go" inwardly, and say to ourselves: "I've done all I humanly can. Now the condition will have to take care of itself."

This mental attitude gives us the feeling of temporary detachment from the trouble and enables our Inner Mind to suggest a way out. When we have been so worried, we have been too close to our problem to see how to solve it. But now the creative power within us, upon our relaxing body and mind, is freed to go to work. It produces ideas and attracts opportunities to us which we would never have recognized if our inner vision had been clouded by depressed and overburdened thoughts.

Happiness cannot be grabbed or selfishly withheld from others. It comes to those who are attuned to the rhythmic ebb and flow of life. Strangely enough, we cannot keep anything by hanging onto it. We must pass it on. You cannot stop a river as it flows onward toward the sea. If you do, that river will overflow its banks and leave devastation in its wake. Everything in life is motion—is moving—is change—is progress. Everything is here for us to use and *pass on.* Your bloodstream is coursing normally through your veins and circulation is taking place. Shut off your circulation, let your bloodstream be checked, and you are apt to pay with your life.

A miser clings to the money he *has,* fearful that he will get no more. His fears steal his happiness of living, eventually destroy his health, and actually keep money from flowing *through* him. You should regard money as a liquid stream, however thin this stream may appear to you at present, realizing that to dam up this stream and attempt to check its flow by hoarding, will cause the stream to change its course and take other channel.

Do not visualize the dollar you have in your hand today as your *last* dollar. It may actually be, at the moment, but there are other moments and other dollars. The harder you cling to the *one,* the more deeply you are impressing upon yourself that it is "the only one." Without realizing it, you are directing this creative power to see to it that this is your last dollar!

I know how difficult it is for you to have faith that other dollars will come—that the flow will continue if you spend that dollar, which seems to be your all, for what you know you direly need. And I know that you can't make yourself do it, the while a certain something inside says, "there goes my last dollar. What am I going to do now? I'm absolutely penniless!"

Forcing yourself to be relaxed isn't going to bring the condition you want. Whenever you have to force a thing it is a sign, as I have said, that you are not sure of yourself-not sufficiently confident that this creative power within you can accomplish, under your direction, what you wish and, on occasion, sorely need.

Every human has daily problems in life. Some are facing their problems resolutely; others are having a struggle; many would do almost anything to overcome a condition if they only knew just how to combat it. But they feel, perhaps as you have felt, defenseless, as though the situation was too much for you—as though you could never regain what has been lost or hope to achieve what you once dreamed of achieving.

When you feel this way, you should take heart from observing the marvelous manner in which the law of the Subconscious Mind is constantly working out in the lives of others. And the best place to obtain such evidence is through a perusal of the daily papers.

Perhaps you may have read the news item from Liverpool, Nova Scotia, which told of Thomas Howell, Chicago financier, breaking the world record for tuna landed with rod and line. The giant horse mackerel tipped the scales at 956 pounds, beating the record of 851 pounds then held by L. Mitchell Henry, English sportsman.

Prior to catching this record-size fish, Howell had pulled in a 792 pounder after it had hauled his small launch two hundred miles in a sixty-two-hour struggle. He thought, at the time, he had landed the biggest fish ever caught in North American waters, but when the news reporters told of the Englishman's catch, Howell said he felt "rather small." Undaunted, Howell said: "Well, the only thing to do is stay in Liverpool until I break the record!"

The following week he brought in a large fish which all in his party thought would be the record-breaker. They watched workmen haul it onto the scales. It registered a "mere" 830 pounds, still twenty-one pounds under the Englishman's record.

Disappointed, but with even greater resolution, Howell said, "Come on! We'll have to go right down and get another one!"

Such a statement revealed the possession by Thomas Howell of a marvelous mental attitude, a natural faculty for concentration-the ability to visualize what he desired to attain despite failure.

The story went on to report Howell's turning his little launch back to Mersey Point and once more letting down his line. It was not long before the biggest fish nibbled and got hooked. The strain of the line kept its mouth open and the fish drowned in three hours and thirty-eight minutes. Landing this fish gave Thomas Howell the biggest thrill of his life, he said, since he could at last claim a world's record!

This actual happening strikingly illustrates how definitely this creative power within may be employed to serve you in all of life's experiences. Thomas Howell, by vividly and confidently picturing himself landing the biggest tuna fish ever caught, gave his Subconscious mind a mental blueprint to follow. It was directed to lead him to the spot where he might hook the biggest fish and Mr. Howell finally achieved his ambition as a result of his *perfect* visualization!

When you consider that many sportsmen have tried for years to catch a bigger fish and thus be proud holders of a record catch, Mr. Howell's demonstration becomes all the more remarkable as evidence that we can command this inner creative power to do our bidding.

Mr. Howell did not take his failures too seriously. He *played* at getting the thing he very much desired. He played with an earnestness and an enthusiasm and a confidence that would not be denied. There was not the slightest trace of worry or fear that he wouldn't be able to catch the biggest fish. In his own words, after two failures, he said, "We'll have to go right down and get another one!"

If you could maintain such optimism in the face of disappointment and discouragement, you would not long remain in your present state. If you could see beyond your troubles and hardships and setbacks—see yourself overcoming them—see yourself relaxing and knowing that good things must come in answer to your vivid, confident visualizing of them, your whole life would soon be changed and a new happiness and health would be yours!

As Mr. Howell himself would probably say, "There's lots of big fish in the ocean still to be caught!" To which I would add: "Decide upon the kind of big fish you want and go after it in the same enthusiastic, visualizing manner that Mr. Howell did and you'll soon have this fish on your line—landing the thing in life you most desire!"

(*a*) The Fear of Growing Old

Are you afraid of growing old?

No doubt quite a number who will read this book have already reached the age which the world considers old. Many have had to make the usual mental adjustment, resigning themselves to the knowledge that they cannot physically do what they once did. Others may be rebelling against this natural ageing of their body and fearing the coming of each tomorrow since it means, to them, a furthering of the dreaded process of growing old. I have had young people tell me that they only wanted to live fifteen or twenty years longer since they didn't want to grow old and be a burden to anyone and there didn't seem to be much fun in living beyond fifty or sixty.

Young people who feel this way have a wrong idea about life and its fundamental purpose. They are not basically interested in real development of character and ability. They are living but for the moment, selfishly desiring to take everything they can out of life without putting any more into life than is absolutely necessary. Young people with such an attitude, are burned out, physically and mentally, at middle-age, and have experienced, as they think, all life's thrills.

They have lived a shallow, superficial existence and when this sort of life has passed them by—when the artificial world they have created bursts like a bubble—they can see nothing in life worth living for. Many such young people do not even wait for middle-age. They are bored with living in their early twenties or thirties and desirous of ending it all.

This is one of the tragedies of our modern civilization— the speed at which we are living. Most of our youths are having experiences shot at them so fast that they cannot begin to absorb these experiences. As a consequence, they make many costly mistakes; they get involved in personal difficulties; they become disillusioned; they try to adopt a "don't care" attitude; they decide that it's no use trying to preserve any ideals—that one had better eat, drink and be merry if one hopes to capture any of the temporary joys of this life. And the result is a pathetic and ever-increasing number of misfits, of young people who have grown old prematurely, who have aged before their time, who have missed the real meaning of life itself and see nothing ahead but a mocking repetition of what has gone before.

To me, the plight of these young people is much more sad than that of a middle-aged person who suddenly awakens to the realization that he or she is getting along in years and apparently can't do anything about it. It is sadder because the average middle-aged person's past life has been rich in experience. Just how rich, many individuals may not themselves have appreciated. Their lives, to them, may have seemed quite routine and humdrum; and yet an outsider might view with envy the experiences of which these lives have been comprised. And any middle-aged person can, when he or she has attained true knowledge of self, draw upon this ripened past experience to build a happy future.

But young people who have lived thoughtlessly, and without purpose, approach later years much like a nutshell which contains only a dried-up kernel in place of the matured fruit which should have been there. You get out of life exactly what you have put into it; and you realize this more and more as you reach greater and greater maturity.

My grandmother, Mary A. Morrow, was a remarkable woman physically, mentally and spiritually. She lived to be eighty-three and was active all her years until but a few days before her passing. She said to me upon one occasion, "You know, it's so hard to grow old gracefully." And yet Grandmother Morrow was setting a marvelous example of doing that very thing. She had a deep and abiding faith in God, in the universe, in the fundamental rightness of things. She bore such afflictions as came to her with a rare patience and fortitude which was expressed in a clipping that she had treasured and which I came across after she had gone. It said, "Life is a battle. We all have a work to do. We must not expect to sail to Heaven on flowery beds of ease; while others fought to win the prize and sailed through bloody seas."

Grandmother Morrow believed that happiness must be *earned*, both here and hereafter. Yet, when her time came to go, with loved ones gathered about her bedside, clinging to her, she was able to face this supreme moment and to say, "You who love me, do not hold me here. I want to go. There are many dear ones over there. It will be a happy release."

None of us needs fear this natural process of growing old who can see this life as a training school for greater things beyond. We should not think of the end as "the end" but only as a new beginning. And though each of us must face this last experience alone, it is comforting to know that dear ones have faced it before us, that untold millions have met the great adventure, and that Science is joining hands with the religions of the world in saying: "One of these days your faith that there is life after death may be proved in our laboratories! We know, beyond a doubt, that a constant evolution of physical forms is taking place. And it is equally possible that there is also an evolution of the soul!"

To fear growing old is to invite misery and unhappiness. The infirmities of old age which have come to some, are very trying, I know. An elderly friend of mine recently said to me, "I hope that I'm taken before I lose possession of any of my faculties." It is the desire of elderly people not to be a physical burden to younger members of their family. As long as they can be up and around and helping in their way, they are happy. But there is a natural dread of being bedridden or unable to do even the little things that would bring such joy. Fear of such an eventuality certainly will not help and may even attract it.

If you are one who is now afflicted, you have the opportunity of testing your own character which you should have developed through the years. You have the opportunity of proving that your inner consciousness, the real you, *your soul,* is the ruling power in life—that it is strong even though your body may be weak. You have the opportunity of demonstrating a courage, a patience and a cheerfulness which should be an example to your children, your loved ones, and which should make their care of you a pleasant duty.

You should not feel badly or look upon yourself as a burden. Every experience that has come to us in life has a reason behind it, if we can but discover it. If you are old and afflicted, the care you are to others may be doing something fine to them; it may be bringing out an element of self-sacrifice, devotion and certain stronger qualities in them which might not otherwise have developed. It is *not* that you *had* to be physically handicapped in order that others might be helped by their right attitude toward your condition but, since your life has worked out in this manner, your dear ones have the opportunity of meeting the situation in the way that *they* should; even as *you* have the opportunity to bear your affliction with fortitude and the faith that this creative power within will not desert you; this God-force, if you so choose to interpret it, will remain with you through whatever changes are to come.

Personally, although I am still comparatively young, I can anticipate my years beyond sixty when they arrive, as an opportunity to survey more leisurely the passing scene; as a chance to judge the ways of men in the light of my more mature experience and judgment; as a chance to go even deeper into the mystery of my own being and its relation to the universe; as a chance to read and re-read the finest thoughts of men, thus enriching my own life that much more; as a chance to serve my fellow humans which the rush of earlier years has perhaps prevented; as a chance to recapture my younger days in devotion to possible grandchildren.

Old age offers so many fine opportunities that the pressure of more youthful and less worthwhile activities denies to us. Of course, our mental attitude must be right; we must look for these opportunities and make whatever physical and mental adjustment is required when the time comes ; but no matter what our position, we should be able to keep mind and heart busy.

A man of sixty related to me that a woman of eighty had congratulated him on his sixtieth birthday, explaining her congratulations by saying, "You have begun to live after sixty years of preparation and are now wise enough to govern yourself and help others. For this reason, you are destined to discover, as I have, that the best part of life is between sixty and eighty."

Life is what you make it, and this is true at any age. Do not fear growing old. Look for the joys and deeper satisfactions which can be yours as life ripens—with each year of experience. Mentally picture yourself as approaching not the end, but a new beginning. Such an attitude will change your entire outlook toward the future. Life must be lived and, at times, *endured,* but it offers us, fundamentally and eternally, the promise of higher and finer things!

(*b*) **The Fear of Death**

I have had many persons ask me how to banish thoughts of a great personal grief which seems, as they say, to be a "fixed idea" with them.

Personal grief, brought about by the death of a loved one, calls for one of the most difficult physical and mental adjustments required of humans. The only way to remove this fixed idea of loss is to realize that this change, which we term "death," comes to us all in its own due time. It must be only a few years at the most, before you and all of us will have joined our loved ones.

This loss may have necessitated certain vital changes in your mode of living and your relation to others. But the greatest tribute you can pay to the one who has gone on is the courage and faith with which you meet the situation. You should visualize this loved one as still alive.

Many families have separated, the children crossing the ocean and growing up, never seeing each other again. In some instances they keep in touch through correspondence, but in others all communication is lost. And yet there is no sense of real personal loss because there is a knowledge that their loved ones still live and have their being in another part of this world.

It will help you to feel that life is continuous, even though you may have lost the physical evidence of its existence; and your sense of loss will be softened if you picture your dear one as though he or she is only separated by an ocean, in this case the ocean of Time. You will look forward, then, to the occasion of rejoining your loved one after your own life experience here is ended. And your thoughts, instead of looking backward upon unhappy moments in your past, will look forward to a time of even greater happiness.

Sometimes associated with a personal grief or the impression that the death of a friend or relative has left upon one's mind-is the strong personal fear of death itself. Here is a typical example of such a fear, expressed in a letter to me:

"I am twenty-eight years of age and I have a terrible fear of death. It seems it is always on my mind. I simply cannot enjoy life or find interest in anything because of this fear. I have had this feeling of fear for eight years. It seems to have me in its grip and I cannot forget it. I am married and have a nice home and a wonderful husband, and I am an expectant mother. My husband can't understand why I don't like to stay at home the way he does, but I can't tell him how I feel. Can you tell me how to overcome this terrible fear?"

My answer to this woman was as follows:

"I can thoroughly sympathize with, and understand your feeling. There are few sensations so absolutely demoralizing, so inwardly agonizing, so physically depressing, as the constant fear of death. This fear, as you say, remains in the background of your consciousness, no matter what you're doing. It is with you in your working hours, and at night it's like a stab in the dark whenever you are aroused from sleep.

"This fear of death may have developed from a number of causes. You may have suffered the loss of a loved one, which has left its deep impression upon you, and your thoughts of them had led to your picturing the possibility of your own death. But, in your particular case, I'm of the belief that your fear has been the result of your being afraid that the happiness, now yours, is too good to last. Many women experience an emotional change after marriage, and you've been so comparatively happy that you've wanted to protect yourself against anything that might cut short this happiness. Because death is the most drastic change that could occur, you've somehow felt that this is the only enemy with the power to destroy the happiness which is now yours.

"The fact that you are an expectant mother has also tended to intensify this fear which exists in the background of your mind, no matter what you may be doing. It prevents you from relaxing and causes you to want to keep constantly 'on the go.' But this fear of death is nothing you can run away from. It must be met, face to face, and put out of your life once and for all.

"These months just ahead of you should be happy and filled with joyous anticipation of the new life to come. Death is not a destroyer unless we make it a destroyer. If you are in normal health at present, and if you free your inner mind of the fear that you've constantly been picturing, death can have no hold upon you.

"You are still young, with the promise of a full lifetime of good things ahead of you. You should realize that you are part of a great creative power which is now assisting in the creation of a new life a creative power that knows no death—a creative power that is ready and willing to respond to whatever mental command you give it. This creative power exists behind all physical things in this Universe. You should learn to rely upon it and to realize that you, yourself, cannot die.

"Your thoughts have been centered upon your physical being, which is only the external expression of your *real* self. Just think, this little new life that you are treasuring within your body apparently did not exist some few months ago! And yet, miracle of miracles, it *did* exist as a potential human identity in the great creative scheme of things. If this were not so, life itself could not manifest.

"From this illustration I want you to understand that, before you were born you apparently were not, and yet you now *are!* The ancient philosophers, wise in their study of life, have said that 'end and beginning are dreams.' From this day on, banish all fear of death. It is but an incident in the great adventure of life, and life was meant to be enjoyed to the fullest.

"If you are alive and happy today, that is enough. Tomorrow never comes until it *is* today. There's no reason why each succeeding day should not be ass happy, or happier, than your yesterdays, if you mentally picture a continuation of this happiness in your future."

CHAPTER SIX

Self Pity

It is very easy, when things seem to be going against you, to feel sorry for yourself. You can probably remember certain times that you have given in to despair, disappointment or humiliation and have then tried to soothe matters by sympathizing with yourself—indulging in what might better be termed, Self Pity.

Self Pity is one of the worst mental habits you could possibly form. Self Pity weakens your resolution, makes allowances for your faults, causes you to place the blame for what has happened upon other people and robs you of your self-respect. Self Pity develops imaginary illnesses in order that you may explain to yourself and to others why you couldn't meet a certain situation.

"If I'd only been feeling myself," you have heard friends say, who are slaves to Self Pity. "I'm sorry I had to fail you," they will go on, "but I was really in no condition. I didn't sleep the night before. I'd worried myself sick. I tried to do too much. . . . If it hadn't been for this other thing happening. . . . I was really counting on Mrs. Jones to help me. . . . Why, I didn't understand that I was to handle *everything!* . . . Well, if I'd only known you expected me to do *that!*"

These and countless other weak-kneed explanations are constantly being offered by men and women who are unconscious victims of Self Pity. They are never directly responsible for anything that happens. There is always something that comes up which is beyond their control and which enables them, as they think, to cover up their own weaknesses and inability.

There is not one of us who has escaped the temptation to sympathize with our lot in life. It is human nature for us to want to "baby" ourselves, to "let ourselves down easy" as the saying goes, to wish to pose as something we are not. But the penalty we ultimately have to pay for petting and pampering ourselves is always very damaging and costly.

You know inwardly if you have permitted Self Pity to take possession of you. And it will do you good if you will subdue your false pride and admit to yourself that you have been shielding your weaknesses rather than trying to overcome them. Simply saying to yourself : "It isn't true. I don't sympathize with myself," will not protect you if your inner self knows differently. You cannot kid this inner mind of yours. It knows instinctively how you feel about things and it follows your real feelings-not your pretended ones.

That is why, when you try to make your friends believe you are not afraid of a thing when you actually are, that your Subconscious mind is uninfluenced and reveals your fears when a situation arises that calls for courage. The brave man or woman does not have to tell how brave they are. They *possess* courage; this quality is a part of them and is something that cannot be put in words.

We all like to believe that our tasks in life are harder than any one else's. This makes us feel stronger and more capable by comparison. It also gives us an alibi when we fail in our accomplishments since it enables us to say: "Well, if So and So had gone through what I have, he or she wouldn't have done as well." There are actually thousands and thousands of people whose main joys in life consist of their reflections to themselves that "other people couldn't have done as well." They have never experienced the vastly greater joy of real accomplishment but have been satisfied to gloss over their failures until they appear to be triumphs in their own minds!

Self Pity is often a carryover from childhood. You may have felt that certain brothers or sisters were favored over you and you have gone off by yourself to sulk about it and to meditate upon the injustice of it all. Perhaps your childhood was actually unhappy; perhaps your lot in life was really hard; perhaps few people ever took a sympathetic interest in you—and so you, in self defense, commenced to sympathize with yourself. But, whatever the cause, you were unconsciously doing yourself definite harm.

Occasionally men and women, who have previously felt strong and self-reliant, have developed Self Pity after suffering financial and physical reverses. This is a throwback to early childish reactions and, once its cause is discovered, can be overcome. But few persons, suddenly seized with Self Pity and a collapse of their morale, realize why they should have such a reaction. They do not understand how a calamity of one kind or another may awaken a long-buried emotional condition which they had all but outgrown but which was still alive in their Subconscious or inner mind.

To be brutally frank with yourself is a difficult attitude to develop until you begin to appreciate the benefits to be derived. The ancient wise men knew the profound value of being able to detach themselves emotionally from their own situation in life and view themselves as though they were an outsider looking on, without pride or prejudice.

You can eliminate the curse of Self Pity and gain a new hold upon yourself if you will resolve now to see yourself as others see you. By this, I do not mean to rely upon the opinions of others or to be sensitive to their viewpoints. But I do mean to visualize yourself as two individuals so that you can get outside yourself and look back upon this *real* self, judging your own thoughts and emotions without permitting them to influence you one way or the other. In this manner, you will be able to put your finger on your weaknesses. You will be far enough removed from the hold your weaknesses have upon you to say to this Inner Self: "I've put up with certain conditions as long as I intend to. From now on, I'm going to show myself no sympathy. I'm going to eliminate the fears and worries and faults which should have been removed years ago. I'm going to face things as I know I should have faced them. If I don't succeed at first, I'm not going to weaken myself still further by inventing new alibis.

"I'm going to discover the reason for my failure and correct it so that my next effort may be more successful. I know now that I've been tying my talents and my inner creative power up in a knot by this attitude of Self Pity. I know that my life has been uncertain and unsettled because I've kept myself from really meeting things. My pride has been partly to blame. I haven't wanted to confess my shortcomings to my friends and I've thought I could keep them from realizing my faults and weaknesses. But my friends have known all along and have been making allowances; and I've been paying a frightful penalty by thinking that I could *kid* myself and others.

"From this moment on, however, I'm a new person. I don't have to carry out this pretense any longer. I feel mentally and physically better than I've ever felt in my life. I know I can do things I've never done before. I know I can soon learn how to call upon this creative power within-and I'm going to discipline myself as a general would discipline a soldier. No more misplaced sympathy or Self Pity. This belongs to the weak, not the strong!"

Such a mental talking to yourself will leave a vivid impression upon your Subconscious or inner mind and enlist its aid in helping you break the hold, once and for all, of your tendency toward Self Pity.

If you are a wife, you will now assume your household duties with a new and radiant spirit. You will take your burdens, however heavy, much more lightly. You will not weigh your husband down with complaints and sorrowful stories when he comes home from work after a hard day at the office or on the job. If your husband is not employed at present, your new, uncomplaining attitude will help restore his spirits and help you both mentally picture better times

If you are a husband, you won't alibi your failure to receive a wage increase or a promotion because So and So had a better "in" with the boss. You won't tell yourself how little what you are doing is appreciated by your wife and family. You won't be saying, "I'm getting nowhere! What's the use of going on like this?" Instead, you will take what might be termed a *hard-boiled* attitude toward yourself. You'll say, "I've had enough of this mollycoddling business. I might as well face the facts. Things could be a lot better if I only gave them a real chance. I've been down on everything and everybody—figured the world was down on me—and, sure enough, I've gotten one tough break right after another. But maybe I've been doing something that's attracted these tough breaks my way. I know plenty of other men who seem to be getting along. There must be a reason. I'm going to change my attitude toward myself and others and see if it makes a difference. I don't know much about this creative power within me, but I'm going to give it a trial by mentally picturing what I'd like to *do* and *be* and *have* in life, and see if it commences working out that way."

Such an attitude can be taken by every person—married or single, young or old—and I know that conditions will very shortly begin to improve.

Your mind operates mathematically, in accordance with a great mental law. It cannot be impressed too strongly that, when you begin operating your mind correctly, good things begin happening to you! And if you have been the victim of Self Pity, cast this destructive influence out of your life forever!

Its riddance means the dawn of a new happiness and definite material benefits for you.

(*a*) **False Pride**

Do you realize that there is probably no quality you possess which can prove so costly as your pride? I doubt if you have thought of it in just this way before, but let's take inventory and see what your pride has done.

Pride has kept you, many times, from admitting to others that your attitude or actions have been wrong. Pride has kept you from confessing certain weaknesses to yourself. Pride has caused you to high-hat or slight certain people, considering yourself superior to them. Pride has caused you to want to be better dressed than Mrs. So and So or have more money than Mr. So and So. Pride has developed a false sense of values and an exaggerated sense of your own importance. Pride is closely related to individual selfishness and is behind many lovers' quarrels; one person being offended if he or she does not receive the attention desired from the other. Pride is unyielding, always demanding and never tender or considerate. The old saying, "Pride goeth before a fall" is therefore very true. Those who do not learn to control their pride, pay for it in bitter experience.

And right here let me make a distinction between Self Respect and Pride. These are two very different qualities. You have heard friends declare, "I'm proud of my appearance. I'm proud of my family." These feelings of self-esteem are no doubt justifiable. Such people might as well have said, "I'm fond of my appearance. I'm fond of my family." It would have meant almost the same. A respect and an admiration was implied.

But Pride, in its real sense, means conceit, a certain arrogance or disdain, display or show. And no one truly likes a proud individual—one who puts on airs. The strange thing is, many of us have a proud streak in us without realizing it. If we possess a definite knowledge about something, we are often uncommonly proud about it and take every occasion to show off this knowledge to those of our friends whom we may regard as "comparatively dumb." We unconsciously display a certain smugness in our attitude which is secretly resented by others.

"So and So would be all right if he or she didn't think they knew so much," you have often heard persons say.

And, usually, it's the individuals who talk the loudest, in trying to impress you with how much they know, who actually know the least. Their pride, as a consequence, finally betrays them.

But letting your Pride stand in the way of a friendship that has existed for years when you inwardly know you are in the wrong, is Pride in one of its most damaging phases. I have not the slightest doubt but that you have had the experience of losing a friend through stubborn pride. Whatever occurred so hurt your feelings that a something within you would not permit you to assume your share of the blame. You have regretted this attitude on your part but you have never been able to bring yourself to apologize and, as a result, the hurt has lasted through the years.

Before I learned that "thoughts are things," that everything we do or think continues to have an effect upon us, I permitted many wrong impressions and mental attitudes to remain in my mind. But when it dawned on me that my present was being determined by my past deeds and reactions to experiences, I got busy and put forth every effort to undo what I had unwittingly done.

There is a mental or spiritual law behind all life which punishes us when we fail to govern our individual lives in accordance with it. Its punishment is impersonal and automatic. Some of us are so proud that we think we know it all ; we think we can do exactly as we please, take whatever we want whether we have earned it or not; trample upon the feelings of others and scoff at the existence of anything but this material universe.

And yet, everything that we see about us *first* existed in a realm that is invisible to us. Scientists tell us that new worlds are constantly being formed in the vast reaches of space through a spontaneous combustion of various cosmic elements. These elements, once formed through combining in a heat which our human brain cannot begin to imagine, finally cool off and become solid. After thousands of years, forms of life commence to appear. Where do they come from? From this great, invisible, creative universal reservoir!

It is well to impress upon you again that a year before you were born, there was not a person who could have predicted that you would exist. And yet you and your very identity were included in this great scheme of things or you wouldn't be here today. You were actually alive before you were born—alive in the universe—and the incident of your creation simply gave your soul or identity the body or form with which to inhabit this earth!

And yet, many of us, in our conceit and exalted ignorance, pretend to know so much about ourselves. We let our Pride tell us that we don't need any creative force within us to do the things we want to do. Many of us have told our friends, "This idea of our possessing a creative power within us is the bunk! We're nothing but a physical organism with a brain and we haven't any access to a creative function outside of the power to reproduce our kind."

And all the time we have been saying these things, the creative power within has been quietly responding to our mental pictures, bringing to pass just what we have pictured, either for our own good or bad. But we will not admit that a power within has been doing it. We dodge the issue entirely. We are afraid this creative power may be connected with something *religious* or that it is related to an *ism*—and we "haven't time for such things."

But let me tell you frankly—you may interpret this creative power as you please. It operates just as willingly for the churchgoer as the non-churchgoer; it is a God-given force, if you view creation as God-given. And you must certainly admit that the Universe abounds in creative intelligence for you are surrounded with undeniable evidence.

Man cannot explain the mystery of this earth's ball, packed with humanity, shooting through space. He cannot tell where it came from, nor can he tell how we originated or where we are going. And yet he proudly sets himself up as an authority—declares there's no life after death—that there's no God—that the Universe is running down like a worn-out clock—that Man has reached his peak.

Proud and haughty man! How the Universe must be laughing at him: laughing with a tender compassion, an understanding sympathy, since the Universe is older than Time and vaster than Space. The Universe laughing at man because man has looked around and about him but not within himself ; the *one* and *only* place where he may ever find the answer to the riddle of Creation !

Man's physical form must die and his pride with it. But man's *inner self,* which occupies this physical form, possesses that elements of creation itself. And man is one day going to learn how to control and operate these creative elements ; and when he does, the physical Universe is going to respond to his bidding.

If you are inclined to be proud, let me urge you to discover the joy of being humble. Let me invite you to put yourself on a level with the beggar, to rub shoulders with the so-called poor and lowly. Let me suggest that you swallow this pride and go to the friend you have wronged and volunteer to make amends. Get the unpleasant mental pictures off your mind and conscience and notice the immediate lift that will come to your spirit, the new happiness you will experience! Pride only conceals a hurt; it doesn't remove it.

Life is short at the longest. Your proud moments are but meaningless drops of water in the great ocean of Time. You injure yourself by a wrong mental attitude and the Universe goes on just the same. But the creative power in the Universe is always at hand, ready to serve you, if you know how to call upon it properly. I have told you how to picture mentally what you want and you should visualize yourself as being freed forever from the wrong influence of your Pride. Do this and watch conditions about you change for the better. Watch your group of friends rapidly expand. And watch your own self take on a greater humanness and inner happiness which will prove more than satisfying.

(b) The Martyr Complex

I am going to ask a question which you are going to find difficult to admit to yourself. Are you the knowing or un-knowing victim of a *martyr complex?* Do you feel that you have been sacrificing yourself on the altar of someone else's desires? Do you like to pretend that you are carrying burdens which should be borne by others? Do you take a peculiar joy in magnifying every act you do for loved ones in the hope that they will heap appreciation upon you? Are you always telling friends and neighbors of the struggle you are having and the grief you are undergoing and that your husband or wife or mother or father, as the case may be, doesn't appreciate it? Do you go about the house or your work with a pained expres-sion, as much as to say, "Look at me—I'm killing myself to bring others happiness. And they don't so much as say 'thank you.'"

I have run into many people who are suffering from the martyr complex and don't know it. They have fallen into the mental habit of over-emphasizing everything they do; of dra-matizing, out of all proportion, each incident or responsibility which comes to them. Such people are always up against the greatest obstacles: no one ever had it as hard as they; and no one can possibly realize what they are going through. They would like to give you the impression that they are facing things with great fortitude-that they are suffering in silence— but, usually, their every expression and gesture talks louder than words. They are the heroic martyrs of the human race and when two martyrs get together and compare notes, it becomes a martyr society. One sympathizes with the other in his or her form of martyrdom and both take turns denouncing the friends or loved ones who have no conception or appreciation of what is being done for them.

An individual with martyr tendencies is usually a person who is gripped by an inferiority complex and who is trying to get credit for possessing qualities that he does not possess. Such an individual will willingly slave for another whom he respects and regards as a strong character, just to be recognized as a capable character in return. The only compensation that many martyr people desire is the expressed appreciation of those for whom they are practically sacrificing their lives.

"I've worked my fingers to the bone for him," I have heard a housewife say. "But you wouldn't think it meant anything as far as he's concerned."

Of course, each one of us does exactly as we want in life. It may not seem so on the surface; but you can always refuse to do too much for anyone else, if you choose. This is one of the great troubles of those who have martyr complexes; they want to do almost everything for their loved ones, deriving a selfish satisfaction in doing it. They like to tell friends that they wouldn't listen to any other members of the family doing thus and so—they *insisted* on doing it for them. Such a practice is bad from two angles. It is bad for the members of a family to be relieved of responsibilities or duties rightfully theirs; and it is bad for the martyr sufferer to keep "butting in" on activities that should be of no concern to him.

The strange and tragic fact about martyrs is that they imagine their self-imposed martyrdom makes them more beloved by their friends and relatives. Actually, this martyr complex is the very thing that takes the edge off true affection and denies to them the genuine expression of appreciation which is gladly given to the person who does for others as he would be done by—and does not make a show of it.

No one enjoys being reminded time and again of the sacrifices another is making on his behalf. I know a husband, who says, "We can well afford a full-time maid to take much of the drudgery off my wife but she so enjoys reporting to me each evening how she's worn herself out keeping house—as a mark of her devotion to me—that she won't let me make it easier for her. Now can you beat that for downright foolishness?"

Of course it's foolish, but people with martyr complexes have a difficult time seeing just how foolish it is. If this husband had insisted upon a maid, his wife would probably have staged a scene, declaring through her tears that this was proof he hadn't appreciated what she'd been doing for him; that she should be physically able to take care of the house herself and didn't he think she was doing all right; wasn't he satisfied with the way things were going? A real martyr dies hard and men and women who face the threat of having their martyrdom removed from them will fight to retain that which they have grown to love.

Yes, it's unbelievable but true; there are many who actually love to play the role of martyrs. They have done it for so long that they would feel lost without it. They have submerged their own personalities; they have devoted years to unnecessary servitude and privation. And now, at this late date, they have all but lost their ability to let loose and really to know what it means to enjoy life.

Many mothers have become martyrs because of their desire to please their children. And as these children have grown up, trained to let mother do things for them, they have not realized that they have permitted their mother to make what amounts to a servant out of herself. From early morning till late at night, mother is up, attending to the wants of the entire family, and finally dragging herself to bed exhausted but telling herself that she is happy in having answered the needs of all. What a miserable, mistaken tragedy this is! What a distorted idea these mothers have wished upon themselves of what constitutes true happiness! Of course they have unintentionally brought this condition upon themselves but it makes the heartache of the situation no less. And if you, who are reading these lines, have such a situation in your home, may I urge you to take immediate steps to correct it.

Many, who have come to see themselves as martyrs of one kind or another and who wish to attain their freedom, have asked me this question: "I now realize my mistake. But what can I do to change things? The members of my family and friends have accepted me as I am—are leaning upon my services—and it would disrupt things for me to call a halt. Since I've gotten myself into this position, wouldn't it be unkind, even cruel, for me to step out and let others suffer because they have learned to depend upon me?"

To such questions, my answer has been: "None of us, no matter how much we would like to think it, is absolutely indispensable. Perhaps no one could do for others quite as we would do. Many of us would selfishly and sentimentally hope not. But, nevertheless, facing absolute facts in order that we may think clearly and see clearly, if something happened to us—if our time came to leave this world—our dear ones would somehow manage to get along without us. This may seem harsh but it is not. In the last analysis, we cannot live another's life for them. If we try to do it, we only weaken the other person and ourselves. It is an unintentional crime for mothers and fathers to try to shield their sons and daughters from the things in life which they should be facing and conquering at their age. It is imposing an unnecessary and cruel handicap upon a young man or woman to protect him or her from life. Deprived suddenly of the guidance of one or both parents this young son or daughter is *lost;* an easy prey to experiences that should have been met in the normal, understanding, right way had the young person been encouraged to solve his or her own problems!"

If you have been a martyr, summon the courage to face your family and confess it and ask them to help you correct this condition in yourself. Tell them you didn't really wish to impose your viewpoints upon their lives; that you thought you were serving them best by the attitude you were taking but that you realize now the burdens you have been needlessly carrying. You are sure that they will be happier and that you will be happier, freed of this leaning upon one another. From now on you wish to devote yourself to new interests and to develop certain talents and gain certain knowledge of which you have deprived yourself—mistakenly telling yourself that you were making this sacrifice for a loved one.

Explain to those you love that you have discovered life must be lived; we are in this world to profit by our personal experiences ; we cannot progress at the expense of another and we each must ultimately assume our share of the responsibilities and duties of this life. No one appreciates a doormat except as a place to wipe one's feet; and all martyrs arrive at a moment of sad awakening when they realize, too late, how futile, though well-meaning, their martyrdom has been.

So you who are a martyr or who have a tendency in that direction, take hold of yourself from this moment on. A greater happiness awaits you and yours, a greater freedom, a greater physical and mental ability to do the things that really count—and to stand side by side with those you love rather than figuratively and literally crawling about upon your knees.

You should know now how to visualize mentally the things in life you actually desire; and this desire to rid yourself of the martyr complex will impress itself upon the creative power within you, causing it to aid you in throwing off the yoke that you have been wearing for years. Is it worth the effort? You *know* it is!

CHAPTER SEVEN

The Quality of Decision

*L*ack of decision has been the cause of countless failures. Just how sure are you of yourself and your own judgment? In matters of importance which you are called upon to decide, are you wavering, hesitant, uncertain, tortured by a wonderment as to whether you are making the right move or a wrong one?

Life demands that you make decisions about something every day. Some decisions are of little consequence, others can easily change the course of your entire existence. But an inability to make up your mind about a certain situation is worse than no decision at all.

"Conditions have been unsettled with me for a long time," a friend of mine said recently. "I just can't decide what I should do. If I do one thing, I won't be able to do the other—and I'd like to do both."

This friend, if he maintains this same mental attitude, will end up by doing neither; losing out on both projects simply because he lacks the resolution to face an issue and decide upon a course of action.

This creative power within you, it is worth repeating, is powerless to act until you have made up your mind. While your Conscious mind is in an unsettled state, it is mentally picturing this unsettled condition upon what I call "the motion picture screen of your inner mind." And your Subconscious, reacting to this unsettled mental picture, sees to it that this condition is continued in your actual life. You get exactly what you visualize-and an uncertain mental attitude produces uncertain situations and results.

"I don't know where I'm at," I've heard many people say, and they were telling the truth. Wrong thinking had gotten them in a muddle and they were unintentionally picturing themselves in a worse muddle. Telling yourself that you "don't know where you're at" is the surest way to lose control over conditions around you.

Your Inner Mind is like a magnet which attracts to it the things you picture. But you *demagnetize* this marvelous creative force when you lack decision—when you fail to direct your mind on a certain objective—when you shift uncertainly from one thing to another.

Years ago, I read the statement of a handwriting expert who said, "People who sign their names without completing the upstroke on the final letter of their name, *seldom finish* what they start in life. In addition to this, those who do not end their signatures on an upstroke are often pessimistic, inclined to be easily discouraged."

At the time, the statement of this handwriting expert made a profound impression upon me. I examined my own signature and found that I did not give the last letter of my name the proper upturn. According to this expert, this indicated that my character was that of one who seldom finished what he started. I therefore resolved, every time I wrote my name, to be sure I rounded out the last letter. And so, for years afterward, I thought as I was called upon to sign my name, "I finish what I start! I finish what I start!"

The result is, today, I have formed such a strong mental habit of going through with whatever I undertake, that my Subconscious or inner mind will not let me alone until it is finished. It keeps prodding me to keep at it. It makes no difference what obstacle I may be up against; how hopeless a task may look; how little time is apparently left in which to accomplish a job; I have impressed this creative power within me so strongly by saying to myself: "You must help me finish what I've started!" that I feel as though I am harnessed to a dynamo whenever I set my mind upon a certain goal.

Now I do not know that there was any real basis in fact for this handwriting expert to claim that those who do not end the signing of their names with an upward flourish seldom complete a task they undertake. But I *do* know that this handwriting expert supplied me with a marvelous mental exercise through which I was enabled to impress upon my inner mind, time and time again, that I was *one* person who finished what he started!

And if you, who are undecided by nature—who have formed the bad habit of being unable to make up your mind about things—would begin to practice this simple exercise, signing your own name with an upward turn at the end, it will not be long until you will have changed your whole mental attitude and your conditions in life. It may be that you sign your name with an upward turn now, but this makes no difference. It is the value of associating the signing of your name with this idea or resolution that counts—the continued impressing of this resolve to finish what you start on your Inner Mind.

Hereafter, whenever you sign your name, say something like this to yourself: "I'm going to know what is *best* to do and I'm going to *do* it. Not only that, whatever I start, I'm going to *finish!*"

The force gained through repeating this resolution will break your undecided mental habit and give you a new, firm, confident hold upon yourself.

Decide on your course of action and stick to it. You will make some mistakes because the right decision must be based upon good judgment; but you will learn to extract a constructive lesson from any well-intentioned mistakes and profit by it in your future. Those who possess the quality of decision, *magnetize* conditions about them and attract things to them. I have given you a mental exercise which will aid you in developing this ability to decide.

The making of your own life is really up to you! What will you decide to do about it?

(*a*) Overcoming Inferiorities

More humans probably suffer from some form of Inferiority than all the rest of the mental complexes combined. Many of us, having lacked the ability for self-analysis, may have been shackled by a sense of inferiority with regard to certain persons or things all our lives without realizing it.

"I don't know why but I just can't meet people," you have heard friends say.

Other characteristic comments which indicate the existence of an Inferiority complex, are:

"I can't see what anyone sees in me."

"Oh, there's no use of my trying. I could never hope to do as well as that."

"I'm afraid of what So and So might think."

"That's too much responsibility for me. I'd rather stick at the job I'm on."

"Yes, I love her—but I could never be worthy of her."

"You may think I'm the man for the place but I'm not so sure. I've never done quite this kind of work before and I wouldn't want to fail you."

"It's a funny thing, but every time So and So speaks to me, I never know what to say."

Such expressions as the above, stamp the individuals as being accustomed to comparing themselves unfavorably with other persons or situations.

You may trace the origin of most inferiority complexes back to your childhood. Parents are often unconsciously the cause of their development. They may have a child who possesses unusual talent and whom they favor because of it. Other sons and daughters, observing this favoritism, consequently imagine there is something lacking in themselves. Such imagining stunts their own mental growth and instills in these children overwhelming feelings of inferiority.

In actuality, every child of normal intelligence possesses rare Subconscious gifts which, if they could be discovered and developed, would be a source of joy to the parents and the "making" of the child.

Poking fun at a childish effort before company is an adult prank which should be discouraged since every child is basically sensitive by nature where older people are concerned. Being ridiculed only serves to emphasize, in the child mind, the gulf of wisdom and experience which is between itself and an adult. By unfortunate comparison, the child realizes its own inadequacy without, at the same time, being able to reason the years that are accountable for the difference. An inferiority, thus developed, becomes Subconscious and persists even after its origin has long since been forgotten.

There is perhaps no mental feeling so uncomfortable as the imagining that others are saying things behind your back or thinking things about you that are critical or unkind. In most instances, there is no foundation in truth for such a feeling which is simply the hangover result of early years when it was "better to be seen than heard" and when to be heard was very apt to invite unfeeling criticism.

Adults too seldom realize how impressionistic children are to everything that is said or done to them. Failure to consider the problems of a child with proper seriousness and on the level of the child's own consciousness, plants the seeds of inferiority. A boy, with a natural talent for drawing, may exhibit a crude picture to his father which, to the boy, is "perfect." His father, in place of regarding the drawing from the viewpoint of his son, sees it as the product of immaturity and inexperience, offering a careless, perhaps absent-minded criticism. By so doing he has "killed" or dulled something potentially fine inside his boy—a creative instinct seeking expression. His thoughtless comment has succeeded only in over-impressing the son with a sense of his own actual incompetence.

Children should not be judged as the world judges. That boy was right in his feeling that the drawing he had created was "perfect." It was as perfect as his developed artistic faculty could produce at the time. Perhaps, if he had repeated this same drawing a week or a month later, it would have represented a higher state of perfection because of added experience in drawing. And, in the light of this greater experience, the boy himself would have been able to recognize what had now become his "imperfection" of yesterday. But what the boy needed, for the sake of unrestrained creative expression, was to be able to feel within himself that his drawing represented "the best" that he was then capable of conceiving and executing.

No one, boy or man, can do his best if the effort is *self-conscious* or accompanied by a feeling of *self-depreciation*.

Ability to analyze, at the moment of conception, the merit of one's work, comes with long training. Until such an ability is achieved, it is important that you believe in yourself and what you are doing while actively engaged. This belief lends a vitality and a sureness to your every thought and move which raises the quality and effectiveness of your result. A sense of inferiority, on the contrary, devitalizes and destroys.

Permit no one to take away your belief in yourself. Without faith in yourself, you will lose control of mental and physical faculties that might, otherwise, carry you to a high degree of accomplishment. Faith is the generator that stirs your Being to its depths and calls forth the best within you. Faith gives intensity and conviction to your mental pictures of success, health and happiness. It is the "developing fluid" of your mind, the invisible chemical that unites your present achievement with your dreamed of future attainment. As long as faith in yourself is preserved, inferiority cannot exist.

One of our most common and, at the same time, one of our greatest mistakes, is to compare ourselves with our fellow humans. Comparison inevitably leads to overwhelming feelings of inferiority. If you are a woman, you feel that Mrs. Better Dresser outshines you. She may be inferior as a person but, since you recognize her as wearing superior clothes, she causes you to feel inferior on both counts. A man may feel that the man above him is a superior person because of the position he occupies, yet this is not necessarily the case. The one who suffers this feeling may actually possess greater ability, the capacity to go much higher, but a capacity which he fails to exercise due to this constant tendency to under-rate himself.

While the right kind of self-analysis is of great value to you, a *self-conscious* appraisal of yourself is ruinous since it combines an emotional and mental reaction to a situation or individual which blurs and distorts your logical perspective. While in such a state of mind you cannot arrive at a true estimate of yourself or your ability.

If you think, for instance, when you are meeting a distinguished person, "I wonder what he is thinking of me? I wonder if I look all right? I wonder what I should say to him?" you are most certainly being dominated by a sense of inferiority.

Turning your thoughts inward at this juncture is just the reversal of what should be done. Your thoughts, instead, should be upon the person you are meeting. No mental picture of his importance and your comparative insignificance should be entertained. You should realize that, whatever this individual's reputation, he is still just a man—and human, like yourself. If you are minus a reputation, it does not follow that you are minus brains or character or personality or the possession of certain worthwhile qualities which this man will appreciate. Stop and think a moment. If you had met this man, not knowing him to have been an important personage, you would then have regarded him as an equal mentally and would have sensed no feeling of inferiority!

Interest in another begets interest. The fear of being unable to keep a conversation going, which comes with some sensations of inferiority, can be instantly dispelled by your asking several pleasantly-phrased questions of the man you are meeting; which questions require that he talk about himself or his activities. Find out as much as you can before meeting him, if it is possible, so that you can be prepared to start the ball of conversation rolling, easily and naturally.

No human on earth can resist the compliment of a genuine personal interest being taken in him by another. If you are struggling against a feeling of inferiority, practice starting others to talking about themselves; practice "drawing them out" on different subjects; discover their hobbies, their special interests, and wherever these hobbies or interests dovetail with yours, expand upon them, making comments of your own. It will not be long before your interest in the discussion itself will cause you to forget any self-consciousness, any feeling of inability to "hold your own."

You will be surprised at your own power of expression, once the repressing influence of your inferiority complex has been removed. The fixation of your Conscious attention upon yourself instead of upon the other person is always disconcerting. Only in complete *un-self-consciousness* can you be your *real* self, and this mental state is attained by the simple focusing of your thoughts upon other persons and things.

A friend who had always been shy and retiring; who had imagined himself to be incapable of doing anything in a public way, was appointed on a City Relief Committee. Compelled to make addresses before the various civic luncheon clubs, he discovered that he was naturally gifted for public speaking. With this discovery, following a period of nervous apprehension, this friend broke the shackles of his inferiority complex and blossomed out into one of the town's most public-spirited citizens.

Development of your own individual expression and way of looking at life is vitally important if you wish to attain outstanding recognition! An attempt to ape what appear to have been the methods used by others who have achieved success, cramps your own natural Subconscious "style" of approaching a like project and invites a growing sense of inferiority as you compare each struggling step with that of those who may have taken the same step more effectively.

Stand upon your own feet and go forward in accordance with the dictates of your own consciousness!

So long as a sense of inferiority lurks within your mind, it will leap out at you when least expected or desired to embarrass and confuse you. This complex can actually hold you back from great attainment, therefore do not delay in taking action to free yourself from it.

Persevere—and one day you will laugh at the ridiculous mental inhibitions which you formerly took so seriously that they kept you from expressing your real self and, as a consequence, withheld from you some of the finest and happiest experiences in life.

CHAPTER EIGHT

The Need of Real Understanding

*T*o have an understanding friend or relative is to possess one of the greatest treasures that this life has to offer. True understanding softens every blow that comes to us; it makes us strive mightily to overcome our faults since the "understanding one" is willing to overlook or forgive them; it provides a haven of refuge when a cold and unfeeling world has temporarily turned its back upon us; and it inspires us constantly to try and try again to make something worth while out of our lives—simply because one friend or relative believes wholeheartedly and unquestioningly in us. This is all that matters—one understanding soul to whom we can unburden the innermost secrets of our heart, confide our most precious aspirations, confess our failings, our misgivings and our weaknesses without fear of censure or exposure.

It does you an immeasurable amount of good to be able to get things off your mind through confiding them in someone you can trust. If you can unload your disappointments and failures and discuss your innermost thoughts with a friend or relative, you can keep these mental pictures from impressing themselves too strongly upon your Subconscious mind. But if you have to hold these mental impressions of your troubles and obstacles because you have no one to whom you can tell them, then they are going to grow stronger as you repeat them to yourself until they will have a bad effect upon you.

Life was not meant to be lived unto yourself; life was meant to be shared. That is the principle upon which the Universe was founded; the positive elements of the Universe are of little use without the negative; and the negative elements are next to powerless without the positive. But join the two together and you have an inexhaustible dynamo of power, vitality and creative energy. This was the intent behind the male, as the positive human element, and the female, as the negative human element; but failure to understand their real purpose and function has, thus far, caused much misery and unhappiness in the union between men and women.

True understanding of each other and themselves has been the one great human need down through the centuries. But the vast majority of men and women have mistakenly believed that they existed only in an outer or physical world and have not learned to tap the marvelous inner resources which each possessed and which could have built for them the indescribable joys that are reserved only for those who have discovered the meaning of true love and how to give it expression through their lives.

You would think that two people, as closely related as husband and wife, would have developed a true understanding of one another, would have learned to know each other's minds—inmost desires, the things that unconsciously offend and which, therefore, should be avoided—as well as the things which just as strongly attract and which, for that reason, should be cultivated. But, instead, we have evidence on every side of men and women constantly irritating one another, of bickering and quarreling and jealousies and suspicions; plainly indicating that there is little or no real understanding between them.

You have the spectacle of wives divorcing husbands and husbands divorcing wives—claiming incompatibility, they can't get along. And yet each, in his or her feverish search for the right mate, hopefully marries again, only to go through the same unhappy experience—never seeming to realize that the trouble is fundamentally within themselves. And, until they correct this trouble, they cannot be truly happy with anyone.

And when you consider the difficulties that members of a family experience in getting along with each other, is it any wonder that we still have wars and rumors of wars?

If there are any individuals who should understand and love one another, it is those comprising the family group. Yet how many families that you know actually enjoy a harmonious relationship?

Brother is often out of sympathy with brother, son is at odds with father, sister cannot agree with sister, and daughter has little in common with mother. The variations of discord are many and the reasons for discord are usually childish.

Basically, of course, our inability to understand *ourselves* has made it next to impossible to understand *others*.

(*a*) **How to Get Along with Others**

Selfishness, greed, jealousy, conceit and prejudice are emotions which enter destructively into our relations with our fellow men. Many of these emotions within us exist as racial instincts which we unwittingly fan into intensity through new experience. Religiously inclined people in the early days had no way of explaining their uncontrolled emotions except by interpreting them as "the works of the Devil" and the declaration that we were "born in sin."

But let us give the Devil his due. He does not exist as a personal being. Therefore, we cannot alibi our sins by transferring the blame for them to some Satanic force. We, alone, are responsible for the carryover of emotional impressions developed through past abuse of Universal Law. And it is strictly up to us, in our association with our fellow humans, to subjugate these elemental feelings, converting our emotions into constructive channels.

Your inability to get along with another is very largely due to your inability to adjust yourself to his viewpoint. With human life and consciousness as it is at present, you cannot expect others to adjust themselves to your viewpoint. It then becomes necessary, if you would gain an insight into the workings of their minds and hearts, that you make your own mind and heart receptive to their outlook.

Blot out all prejudice within your own consciousness. Prejudice is so easy to develop, under stimulation of wrong emotions, and so exceedingly difficult to erase, once it has become established. But as you give out-so will you receive. You cannot make true friends of people if you hold yourself in reserve. You must express the real soul of you in your every human contact if you would attract as well as broadcast a feeling of good will.

Recognition that all races have a just place in the great scheme of things and realization also, that all races have certain unfavorable characteristics which they are struggling to work out, will help you in maintaining an attitude of tolerance.

If any of us had reached a stage of perfection, there would be no reason for our being in this plane of existence. The operation of Universal Law would automatically unite our consciousness or ego with an incomprehensibly higher state of being. That we are where we are should humble us into "judging not that we be not judged." We all have our faults. Refusal to admit these faults and to attempt to correct them, makes it that much more difficult for us to expect fair treatment and consideration from others.

You will find few persons, ultimately, with whom you can place yourself completely in tune. This is because we all differ so widely in soul development. Our grades of consciousness are as variant as the crystal formations in snowflakes. We are constantly melting into new designs of greater beauty or ugliness, dependent upon the nature of our reaction to external experience. And when two truly congenial and understanding souls meet on life's rough sea, it is the greatest adventure that can come to man or woman.

How many thousands of lonely souls there are who crave but one understanding mind and heart with whom to share the burdens and problems of this world! There are lonely souls in high places and low. A rich man may not be sure of friend or relative, feeling that all have secret designs upon his wealth. A poor man is more blessed since sorrow and poverty have reduced his associates to a realization of true values, deprived them of their world of sham and pretense and brought from them a genuine expression of sympathy and brotherly love. But, even so, many a poor man, economically in exile from the things his soul desires, is lonely for companionship not possible under such circumstances.

But, know this—whether rich or poor—you are undergoing whatever you are experiencing now because of a Subconscious inner need. If you are now forced to deal with people for whom you have no respect; if you cannot be sure of the genuineness of certain friends and acquaintances; if circumstances have thrown you in association with humans of different tastes, customs, ideals; life is giving you the opportunity to expand your own consciousness and broaden your own soul by development of a greater humanity for your fellow man.

It never hurts you to be friendly toward another; but it hurts another who would be unfriendly to you.

It has been my experience to have dealt with individuals whom others have warned against as "no good." "They'll let you down; they'll take advantage of you; they'll betray your confidence;" friends have said. But, while some of these associations have ended unhappily, it has not been because the individuals dealt with have failed me. They have, instead, failed themselves.

You will find, if your own attitude is right, that you can establish your own basis of dealing with others. If you regard a business man as none too ethical in his transactions and decide that you "had better *do* him before he *does* you," then you have elected to meet him on his own plane of crooked consciousness. And, unless you are more expert at crooked mental manipulation than he, you are going to get the worst of the bargain.

You can negotiate with this same man, however, and cause him to deal fairly by letting him see that you are not trying to "outsmart" him, that you are willing to give value received. Because you have given him credit for honorable and just business practice, you have appealed to a seldom touched sense of honor within him and he will see to it that whatever business obligations he assumes concerning you, will be strictly adhered to.

Remember—nothing can happen to you in your External life that does not have its potential counterpart in your own consciousness. This being true, you attract or repel people in accordance with the nature of your character and mental attitude.

Since no two humans are exactly alike in viewpoints or backgrounds of experience, you can get along with others only as you call from them the interests that you both possess in common.

I have, for instance, friends who are lovers of sport and other friends who are lovers of music. Whenever I am in the sport mood, I get in touch with a sport enthusiast and live in the sporting consciousness of this friend while in his company. A thorough congeniality is enjoyed because both of us are on the same plane of understanding and appreciation.

A sport lover and a music lover, unless each were interested in both fields, would have little in common. Talking football to many symphony concert conductors would be as futile as talking Greek to a wooden Indian. The mere mention of the sport would be met with a disinterested gesture.

For this reason—because each of us have different motives, different objectives and interests in life—constant human adjustments are required. Humans in the mass can therefore come together only upon the most basic of humanitarian principles. With individual interests so profoundly diverse, and so few humans willing to take the trouble or make the effort to adjust themselves to others, the world has been filled with discord, misunderstanding, hatred, distrust, jealousy, fear and every kind of destructive emotion.

To get along with others requires patience, tolerance, insight, sympathy, helpfulness and understanding. These qualities, freely employed in your association with others, will pay the richest of human dividends.

Start, this instant, correcting all conditions within yourself that are making you unattractive to certain of your friends and acquaintances. You know now how to explore your own consciousness and to determine why certain associations have not worked out happily. You will know, as you study others, whom to avoid and whom to cultivate.

The best way to get along with some types of individuals is to get along *without* them.

You cannot make others over; they must remake themselves. Either you must appeal to the good, constructive side of them and disregard the other while in their company, or have little or nothing to do with them.

This does not mean that you are to show resentment or condemnation of certain faults. If your friendship or association is considered worth while by them, they will realize why it is being denied and, if they care sufficiently, they will make the effort to redeem themselves in your eyes. If they do not, there is nothing that you can do about it. Experience is the only real teacher.

CHAPTER NINE

How to Determine Your Talent in Life

*H*ow often have you heard some friend or acquaintance make a remark like this: "I'd give a million dollars if I could be as talented as Mrs. So and So. Everybody loves her. She's got the grandest personality and she always seems to know the right thing to do and say at the right time!"

And haven't you noticed, when you have heard people make remarks like this, offering a million dollars for something that no amount of money can buy, how unwilling most of them are to give the one thing necessary to be like Mrs. So and So?

That one thing which is required to accomplish something worthwhile in life is *concentration*—the ability and the willingness to visualize, to picture mentally what is desired; and then to back up this picture by putting forth every effort toward its attainment.

Any woman who is talented and attractive and lovable has not acquired these qualities through chance. Neither has she been able to buy them with any million dollars. Behind her appealing personality is probably the story of a woman who sacrificed many ordinary pleasures to develop certain natural talents she possessed. The fact that everybody loves her indicates that she has cultivated a ready sympathy and understanding and genuine interest in others.

She *says* the right thing at the right time because she is in command of herself. She *does* the right thing at the right time because she is not thinking of herself first; she is thinking always of others, anticipating what they would like to have done for them, and *doing* it. All of these factors, which contribute to Mrs. So and So's popularity, are within the reach of every woman—and man. The achievement of talent and popularity depends only upon the *price* you are willing to pay for it in continued effort and visualization.

No human being ever got anywhere by merely wishing for something that others have. It is rare that two individuals possess exactly similar talents and rather than try to imitate the talent of another, you should strive to discover and develop the peculiar talent that you possess which can lead to a success all your own.

You may think, at this present moment, that life has been very sparing with you in the matter of talent. Perhaps you were unable to secure what you consider a good education. Perhaps seeming force of circumstances has kept you from the experiences you feel you should have had to develop the ability you desire. Perhaps you haven't yet discovered any particular talent or leaning which you feel could do much for you in a personal, social or business way. But if you haven't, let me assure you, *that* talent is *there*. It is in you and the problem is to discover it and get it out.

Not a person was ever born who did not possess some talent—some potential ability to do some one thing expertly well, if it was only digging a ditch. And *few* individuals, no matter what walk of life, have ever learned to make full use of the talents with which they have been born. This is because few have learned how to analyze themselves; how to see themselves as others really see them; and, what is more important, how to see possibilities in themselves that no one else can see!

If you can see possibilities in yourself, regardless of the opinions others may have, nothing can keep you from ultimately reaching your goal. Every day, in every part of the world, someone is succeeding whom no one else credited with a chance to succeed. But these persons believed implicitly in themselves; nothing could shake that faith-no amount of hardship or setbacks or turndowns from those who might have helped. The creative power within these persons carried them through to the success that they saw themselves attaining.

You do not need money to start you on the road toward success. You need a *changed mental attitude;* and the money will come. You need to know yourself -to be able to explore your hidden, undeveloped resources-talents which, once liberated and developed, can do for you what the talents of others have done for them.

You can use the formula I have given you for reaching and controlling your Subconscious mind. This will enable you to get next to your innermost thoughts and feelings. It will enable you to sound out what you really want to do—what you really feel capable of doing.

In analyzing yourself, it is necessary that you get away where you can feel free from the opinions and dictates of others. Relax your physical body as I have suggested and make your Conscious mind passive. Then turn your thoughts inward and ask yourself honestly what you think yourself fitted for—in what direction your talents or inclinations lie.

Do not permit your Conscious mind to enter into this meditation. If you do, it will drag in your fear and worry thoughts and any inferiority complexes you may have; all of these things attempting to tell you that you couldn't do what you inwardly want to do, if you tried.

But you are listening now to your Inner Self talking; you are listening with your inner ear to what your Subconscious mind has to say; and this is the part of you that contains everything you hope to be and is the sum total of all you have been up to this present moment. This Inner Self has the right answer to every problem and the way to get this answer is to put aside all your guessing, wondering, calculating thoughts; make yourself quiet physically and mentally; and let your Subconscious mind pass the solution on to your Conscious mind in the form of an idea or a hunch or a strong feeling in a certain direction.

When you are sure you have received the right impression concerning yourself, do not let your Conscious mind talk you out of it. When you are dealing with things you have not yet accomplished, your Conscious mind is apt to warn you: "Better let well enough alone. It's a long, hard job to get to be a person as talented and popular as Mrs. So and So or Mr. So and So; and even if you made the effort, think of the things that might happen to keep you from getting anywhere!"

If you listen to this kind of "talk" from your Conscious mind which is so filled with a consciousness of your failures of the past, you will be doomed before you start.

You have heard friends say many times: "I talked myself out of doing what I really wanted to do. At the time I didn't believe enough in myself. I wasn't willing to take the risk. But if I'd set out right then and followed my own inclinations instead of taking the advice of others, I'd have been where So-and-So is today. But now, of course, it's too late!"

It is never too late to change your position in life materially, whether you be old or young. Some achievements, quite naturally, require a certain length of time to accomplish, a certain physical or mental effort. And while you may have missed out on many fine opportunities, you can still adjust yourself to the circumstances that may surround you and get more out of life than you have thought possible.

Once you have decided wherein your talent or aptitude lies, begin visualizing yourself as a success in this line. See yourself already doing the thing you desire to do. It does not matter that your talent is still undeveloped. Your Subconscious mind will see to it, once given the proper mental picture of success, that the right steps are provided by which this talent can be developed to the point of bringing this success.

You are aware, no doubt, of the difficulty that the average hometown boy often has in achieving success in his home community. This is due to the fact that older people can seldom visualize young men doing the sort of things to which they aspire. Instead, the well-meaning elders classify the abilities of the young, crediting them only with such talents as have appeared on the surface—or such experiences as the young people have had thrust upon them, granting these same young people little or no opportunity to make good in other lines for which they possess much greater native unexpressed ability.

And the irony is that other young people, coming in from outside communities and claiming an ability in certain lines, are accepted on *face value* and given the opportunity to prove themselves in positions for which many home-town young men and women are just as ideally suited. But because of this *set* mental picture of their limitations in the minds of their elders, many of these young people are forced to leave their home communities to achieve the success they desire! This indicates again the power of thought and how sure of one's self everyone must be to meet the tests of life, to know how to make the most from the least, and how to turn what others would consider a liability into a decided asset.

As I have said—you do not have to give anyone a million dollars to *be* what you *want* to be; but you *do* have to give *yourself* a great deal of personal attention. Gaining control over your Inner Self and the creative power you possess is the greatest thrill and pleasure in life as you will soon discover if you have not already done so. And you will not begrudge any time you spend with yourself as you realize the increasing physical and mental profits to be derived.

Character comes with right thinking and the right reaction to the things that happen to you. Talent comes through the intelligent application of your inner resources to the field for which you are fitted. Popularity comes through giving generously of your talents and yourself to those who have earned the right to be your friends. And success comes in the proportion that you have put forth the effort to *deserve* the things you have pictured for yourself.

So start now analyzing your capabilities, determining whether you are getting out of life all that you can, appraising yourself to discover if ,you are doing the thing for which you are best suited, checking up on certain qualities or habits which may be offensive to, others without your realizing it. See yourself devoid of any sugar coating. Do not permit your pride to cover up your defects. Do not attempt to defend your weaknesses to your Inner Self. Make up your mind that you would much rather hurt yourself than let others hurt you. In other words, you would much rather admit to yourself a damaging fault than have it pointed out to you in public.

Your life is yours to make of it what you *will;* but dare to be yourself at all times ; and do not allow any person or force of circumstances to keep you from doing the thing you want *most* to do—for therein lies your greatest possibility of success!

(*a*) **Self-Confidence**

How much confidence do you have in yourself ? Just how sure are you of your ability to accomplish what you want to accomplish? Of course, you may pretend to your close friends and relatives that you are perfectly capable of assuming your responsibilities and, at the same time, you may be having a struggle inwardly to make yourself believe that you are!

I have had people say to me, "I just wish I were the person others think I am!" And when I ask, "Well, why aren't you?" They reply: "I don't know. Everyone seems to think I'm so sure of myself when I'm really not at all. I suffer agony every day wondering whether I'm going to be equal to what I'm called on to do. I'm only glad that no one else notices it."

Now this, you will admit, is a fine state of affairs! And, if you are suffering from a lack of confidence in yourself, you will probably be sympathizing with the feelings which have just been expressed. No doubt these very words might just as well have been uttered by you.

But—granted there have been times and are times when you are none too sure of yourself—let's try to find the reason why.

Your lack of confidence may be traced back to something that happened in your childhood. I know a man who almost drowned when a boy. His mother lived in such fear, thereafter, of something terrible befalling him, that she kept him from the water. Playmates of his age, meanwhile, learned to swim and the boy, feeling keenly not only his inability to swim but his fear of the water which had been intensified by his mother's attitude, developed a sense of inferiority. He wasn't sure of himself; he visualized others getting the better of him; of others being more capable; of himself being practically helpless to do anything about it.

Now let's follow this boy into manhood. Plagued by this near-drowning experience, the effect of which he had never overcome, this man unconsciously developed the same attitude toward everything in life. He was afraid to venture for fear he would get in over his head—afraid the situation would get beyond his depth. Your mind, remember, thinks in terms of mental pictures. You may be under the impression that, because this man was afraid of the water, this fear had no further influence in his life. But, in this impression, you are wrong.

Anything we have not conquered and which we fear, becomes an overshadowing, unconscious influence in our lives. It robs us of our real confidence in ourselves. We instinctively feel unequal to a situation, without being able to explain the exact reason why. But, given an understanding of how our mind really operates, we can go back in memory and recall certain experiences which have been the basic cause of our present reaction.

If you lack confidence in yourself today, you have reacted wrongly to some occurrence in your past. And, until you have discovered the origin of your weakness and removed it, you will be unable to face certain conditions as you should.

Ask yourself what has happened in your life to make you feel afraid of meeting a situation. Did you fail to conquer some little fear in your childhood which made a great and lasting impression upon you? And has this little fear magnified itself into a big fear as time has gone on? Nine times out of ten this is the reason behind your present lack of confidence. And once you have determined the reason it will seem so ridiculous to you—permitting a childhood reaction to steal your self-confidence—that you will resolve to overcome this feeling at once.

You may not be able to throw off the hold that an inferiority has upon you immediately. But each step that you take in the right direction will weaken this hold and help form a new mental picture in your mind's eye. At present your mind probably contains a series of mental pictures in which you failed to meet a certain situation. And every time a similar situation has occurred, you have reacted the same way. There was nothing else you *could* do since your inner mind operates in accordance with the mental pictures you have given it.

You cannot escape the consequences of your past actions by trying to run away from them or to dodge the issue. It is impossible to get away from yourself. And the sooner you decide to "face the music," as we say, the sooner you will be freed from the humiliation and misery caused by your lack of confidence in yourself. We none of us know what it is possible for us to accomplish or undergo until we have put ourselves to the test.

If you can discover the basic cause behind your lack of self-confidence, start to work eliminating it. This man whose life was blighted by his fear of the water should have made it his business to take swimming lessons—to place himself in the competent hands of a swimming instructor, telling this instructor just how he felt and what had happened. Then, through familiarizing himself with the water and, while under the safe supervision of his instructor, this man would have gradually overcome his fear. A victory over the thing feared, a realization that he could now swim as well as his former boyhood friends, would give this man an instant feeling of *equality*. He would no longer have this Subconscious sense of inferiority, as though friends and associates had the edge on him. This new mental attitude would give him greater confidence in his business dealings as well as his personal life.

Self-confidence is one of the most vital and helpful feelings that you can have. It acts like the yeast which, when mixed with dough, causes the dough to rise and take form. Self-confidence, once it permeates your being, gives life and vitality to your plans of success. It develops a *magnetism within,* which helps attract to you the things desired. Those who radiate self-confidence in their own ability inspire the confidence of others. All great leaders are men and women who have impressed their followers that they not only know where they are going but how to overcome the obstacles in the path of getting there!

All great accomplishments first happen in the mind of man. Until a man thinks he can do a thing, he is powerless to do it. But the majority of humans are being troubled by their everyday affairs. You perhaps feel, just at present, that if you could only develop the confidence to meet your daily problems, to look toward the future with the assurance that tomorrow is going to be better than today; *if* even this much confidence could be attained, you would be happy!

This being the case, start *now,* reliving your life and putting your finger on the things that have occurred which, without your realizing it, have destroyed much of your self-confidence. Then, mentally picture yourself as breaking free from these wrong reactions, taking a new stand against these foolish feelings which have been unconsciously holding you back. With persistence, you will soon be able to look the people squarely in the eye whom you've formerly held in awe, and tell them: "Yes, I know I've never done quite this kind of work before, but I'm *sure* I can make good at it. You can *depend* on me!"

I have told you how to draw upon this creative power within. Once you have removed the wrong mental pictures from your consciousness and given this creative power the right kind of mental pictures to act on, your self-confidence will be restored ; and conditions around you will change for the better.

Do not lean on anyone else. Lean on this creative power within. It will never let you down; never fail to respond if you call upon it properly. *Believe* in *yourself.* You hold the *key* within you to all the good things in life!

(*b*) **The Value of Patience**

Just how patient are you? Can you wait for things to happen in their own good time or are you so impulsive, so anxious for them to happen that you try to hurry them up, to force circumstances your way and, as a result, lose the very things you are seeking?

I know many friends who are like this. Without realizing it, they are their own worst enemies. They are so eager to bring a certain condition to pass that they spoil it for themselves and others.

When you plant a seed in the ground, you must wait for the sun and the rain and the nourishing elements of the soil to do their work. The seed does not spring up as if by magic in a few moments of time. It requires days and weeks and often months to unfold the marvelous possibilities within itself. Any attempt on your part to hurry it, to over-do the amount of moisture needed, to make the soil too rich, instead of hastening the seed's progress would retard it and might even stunt the growth or cause it to be poor in quality.

Everything in life has a certain natural rhythm or vibration. You cannot change the tempo of a fox-trot into waltz time and expect it to remain a fox-trot. You cannot heat water beyond a certain point without its becoming steam. You cannot give an automobile too much gas without choking your carburetor. You cannot rush constantly at top speed without eventually suffering a nervous breakdown or a physical disorder.

Get this fact well in mind—the Universe is not in a hurry. It has all the time in the world. Its processes of creation are going on eternally. And we, who have been born with this creative power within us, have acted as though we either doubted its existence or were unaware of it.

Once you know, beyond the shadow of a doubt, that you are actually linked with the Universe—that the creative power within you is the same creative power which pervades all time and space—then a new peace comes over you as you realize that you can lean upon this power; that it will support you, keep your mind and spirit eternally young and fresh. Your body may age, since it is related to this physical world in which you now live; but even your physical being will be so influenced by your new mental attitude that it will grow old gracefully, as fruit ripens upon a tree.

At present, because you do not really know yourself; because you have not learned to draw upon this creative force within sufficiently you are resisting many things in life. You have imagined it was necessary for you to fight for your rights; to go out and get what you have wanted, if necessary by almost brute strength. But this is only the physical way of getting things. There is a better, finer and surer way.

There is a mental law which operates automatically and impersonally. It plays no favorites. It responds to those who know how to operate it for their own good. And this mental law sees to it that everything you have really earned and deserved is brought to you.

Now I know that this statement may cause you to go back over your life and say to yourself, "Is that so? I've earned much more than I've ever gotten out of life. And I've hardly ever received what I've really deserved. And look at the So and So's! Look at the money they have; and did they ever work for it? No, there's nothing fair about this life! You can't tell me!"

But wait a moment. Restrain this impulsive side of your nature. Relax and let's look at life and, your relation to it from an unprejudiced viewpoint. Let's really analyze your situation.

In the first place, it's always a great mistake to compare yourself and your condition to others. How could a person on the outside possibly gain a true knowledge of your own feelings and the effort you have put forth to attain what you have in life? Perhaps an outsider could see nothing on the surface to indicate that you were deserving of what has come to you; and he might say, "Look at So and So—how things fall into his lap! Did you ever see the beat of it? And yet *I* have to work for a living!"

Of course you would resent such a comment because everyone likes to feel that he is entitled to what he has. Make no mistake about it-we all pay the price, physically and mentally, for everything that comes to us in life. And the only *lasting* happiness is the happiness which is attracted by the *right* mental attitude.

Would you change places with a millionaire if you knew that he was ill from overeating or drinking or nerve strain? Would you change places with a rich husband or wife who had everything in life but love and understanding for each other? Would you be willing to sacrifice love of family, home, everything you now hold dear, for *money*?

Be patient! The real things in life cannot be denied you! But get yourself out of the habit of envying other people; of wondering why they apparently have so much and you have so little. Actually, you may now possess more than they. I have known rich people who would have given much of their wealth to be able to live simply, but their position in society prevented it; they could not escape the spotlight. Do you consider this happiness?

Be patient! Let the rich have their wealth. Do not be misled by surface indications of happiness. The rich who are truly happy have earned their happiness by developing the character to master material wealth instead of permitting it to master them. But are *you* master of the present circumstances and conditions surrounding you? If you are not, then all your day dreams and desires to have what you think other people now have, will amount to naught.

Be patient! All fine and worthwhile developments take time. There is an old saying: "Rome was not built in a day."

There is another old saying: "All things come to him who will but wait."

Be patient! An expectant mother carries her child and happily anticipates its arrival for close onto nine months. A man creates an idea for a new business, works at it night and day ; the nights and days stretch into years before a great organization employing thousands of men and women finally results! Everything happens in due course of time.

Be patient! This great country, the United States of America, had the most humble of beginnings. Its early founders were men of vision. They foresaw the America in which we are now living and provided for it in one of the most remarkable constitutions ever drawn.

If you have lost your money, your health, your confidence, your faith—you can get it back, perhaps not all of it in some instances, but enough to bring you peace and comfort and consolation since you will have learned how to live truly and enjoy life.

Learn to relax, learn not to take life too seriously, learn to lean upon this creative power within which builds your mental pictures into realities. Learn to be *patient* because you cannot force this creative power. It will work speedily for you only if your mental picture of what you want is vivid and clear. But if you try to force anything to happen, it is a sign you are afraid it may not happen.

If you really are confident, if you know that you have earned the right to have what you desire, you can be relaxed and patient about it since this creative power will surely bring it to you!

CHAPTER TEN

Success in Life

*I*n this volume it has been my aim to leave you with certain fundamental facts about yourself—a knowledge sufficient for you to develop through practice, the *conscious* control of your Subconscious mind. It is my hope that you now know and understand the key to- the operation of your own mind which will enable you to draw upon this creative power within: to picture mentally the things in life you desire; to know that things first happen in your mind before they can happen in your outer world; and that there is a method by which you can change your entire life and circumstances through seeing yourself, on "the motion picture screen of your inner mind," *doing* or *being* or *having* something that you very much want. If I have been able to leave you with this one great universal fact about your real self, then I know that you have been served through reading this book.

It is, of course, up to you—the use that you make of this knowledge given. I take no credit for being the originator of this knowledge. It is as old as Time, as old as the spiritual or universal laws behind all things. I have put this knowledge into more concrete and understandable form that you might be able to apply it at once and get everyday benefit from the taking on of a new mental attitude. If I have been the medium for the accomplishing of just this much in your life, then I am indeed happy because I know what this same knowledge has done for me and for my loved ones—and that it can do the same for you and yours.

In the presence of this great creative power and the realization of how much it is really doing for us, one becomes most humble. No man or woman can remain conceited or egotistical after they have come to know themselves. The knowledge that we are all basically dependent upon this same universal creative source of supply gives us a feeling of kinship with all things.

We cannot take an attitude of superiority toward those less fortunate and more ignorant than we. Rather it is our duty, when asked, to pass on such knowledge as we know would be of benefit to those who are struggling to learn the truth about themselves.

Life is, or should be, a sharing of the good things with each other. Real joy is in the giving; and since we cannot give anything that we do not possess, we must first have gained either knowledge or wealth before we can share it with friends or loved ones. But knowledge of one's self is wealth—the only real and *lasting* wealth in this Universe.

We're on the threshold of great mental developments. Sir Hubert Wilkins, the world famous Arctic explorer, has told me, "We scientists, with our research expeditions, have pretty generally covered the face of the earth; but one great unexplored area remains—the vast, uncharted realms of the Human Mind!"

As yet, humanity at large has not learned how to think. Today one man does the thinking and makes up the minds of millions. If his thinking is crooked, millions will think crookedly with him. Leaders of thought, therefore, assume a tremendous responsibility in guiding the destiny of Mankind.

It is wrong thinking that has visited the present unsettled, chaotic circumstances upon the peoples of all lands. Only right thinking, followed by right action, can liberate Humanity from the frightful condition that intensified fear, hate, lust and greed has brought about. Many of us have been creating our own ruin by wrong thinking. We have done it by wrong thinking in the home, wrong thinking in business and wrong thinking toward our fellow humans.

But you, who have been given a working knowledge of the one great law of Mind, no longer have any excuse for not knowing why things are happening as they are. You should now be able to predict, to a mathematical certainty, what will result if you do not change what you know to be a wrong mental attitude.

It is imperative that you do not permit yourself to be drawn into the whirlpool of wrong thinking which at times passes over the mass of a people like a damaging tidal wave. The next few years are going to decide the fate of civilization. Whoever you may be—or however humble you may consider your station in life—your mental attitude and the stand you will decide to take in relation to the great changes that are coming is vitally important-to you and to the world.

The time is already short in which to achieve the mental preparedness necessary to meet these cataclysmic changes. Will you commence now, fixing your attention, your desire and your effort upon the attainment of genuine success in life?

Real success in life was meant to be attained on all three planes of your Being-the physical, mental and spiritual. And now, as a final summing up, I am going to picture for you the mental attitude which the well-balanced person should have in life and let you judge for yourself your fitness for starting from where you are to where you wish to be.

Inquire of your Inner Self, as you read, whether it is your attitude:

To regard Life as purposeful.

To accept Life and its conditions cheerfully, no matter what your environment.

To love every human because you are related to all Life and, in exact accordance with your regard for others, so will they think of you.

To recognize this as a rational and an intelligent Universe.

To attain a consciousness that you are vital to the working out of the Infinite plan.

To see in the humblest worker and the greatest teacher, equal possibilities for Service.

To be courageous—resisting the temptation to give up a struggle which seems hopeless—secure in the Faith that Success has always been built out of Failure, that Happiness cannot help but follow Tribulation.

To give your best at all times, putting everything you can into Life, doing right because it is *right*—and not from promise of reward or fear of punishment.

To realize that you beget Failure only when you do not properly use the means at hand.

To feel that opportunity is always present for your advancement—dependent upon the Will you exert to grasp it.

To become acquainted with your Inner Self, thus opening the door to undreamed of achievements.

To appreciate that it is not alone what you *are*—but what you are capable of *becoming*—which should concern you.

To place the right valuation upon the things in Life—wasting little time upon passing fancies.

To conserve your physical, mental and moral forces that they may be directed for personal and public benefit.

To be "thy brother's keeper," knowing that the strong must support the weak.

To follow the beaten path only until you can walk alone.

To be constantly aware that Today is the Opportunity and Occasion of your Life.

To have the fortitude to exact the lessons from Life's experiences as you go along—in order that you may be better prepared to face the Future.

To be a friend for the sheer joy of having friends in return.

To reach out a hand to those who are in the mire of despair, giving them a lift out of pure gratitude for being better off than they.

To rejoice in Life's trials, serene in the knowledge that, whether your portion has been more bitter than sweet or more sweet than bitter, you have fought the good fight—you have been true to the best that was in you. Though to err is human, you have striven always toward the Divine.

In so doing, you have contributed your share toward the world's *progress*—

You have added to the sum total of *human happiness—*

And life has given to you that something more priceless than worlds—*your soul.*

THAT IS SUCCESS!

11038266R00086

Made in the USA
San Bernardino, CA
06 May 2014